THE WOMAN'S DAY
Dictionary of
FURNITURE

THE WOMAN'S DAY
Dictionary of
FURNITURE

General Editor: Dina von Zweck

Illustrations by Helen Disbrow
and Charles H. Rieger

A MAIN STREET PRESS BOOK

CITADEL PRESS
Secaucus, New Jersey

First edition

Text copyright © 1983 by The Main Street Press

Illustrations copyright © 1983 by CBS Publications, The
 Consumer Publishing Division of CBS, Inc.

Published by Citadel Press
A division of Lyle Stuart, Inc.
120 Enterprise Ave., Secaucus, NJ 07094

In Canada: Musson Book Company
A division of General Publishing Co. Limited
Don Mills, Ontario

Produced by The Main Street Press

ISBN 0-8065-0842-6

Manufactured in the United States of America

Contents

Introduction

Furniture is the most useful of antique objects, and furnishing a room with fine pieces from the past among the most pleasurable of activities. Hardly a home in America is without at least a few such heirlooms—a Boston rocker, a Windsor chair, an oak center table, a pine corner cupboard. In recent years acquiring antique furniture has become a passion of millions of people. The supply of good pieces has begun to dwindle, and their cost to rise accordingly. The ability to identify and to set a value on these antiques has now become essential. *The Woman's Day Dictionary of Furniture* is designed to meet these needs in a convenient and economical format. The book is organized alphabetically by form—from beds to whatnots—and includes carefully detailed line drawings of over 700 types of furniture. In addition to information on style, period of manufacture, and characteristic details, a value is indicated for each type of piece, from the simple to the sublime.

The emphasis throughout the book is on the most common pieces of furniture to be found in the North American marketplace today—pieces produced on this side of the Atlantic. Furniture has been made in the New World since shortly after colonies were established in the 17th century. Both the pieces that were made and their decoration followed the styles with which the colonists had been familiar in their native lands. In some categories such as chairs, chests, sofas, and tables, English and French examples are also given. European furniture has been imported for the past 350 years, and the flow of elegant pieces has increased in the 20th century as the demand for antiques has grown. Approximately sixty-five percent of the examples explained and illustrated, however, are of North American origin.

The value of a particular piece of furniture will vary greatly in relation to condition, rarity, and demand. The price of the same object is also likely to be different if it is sold on the East Coast or West. In general, early American pieces command much higher prices than English or European antiques of the same period. Since value can vary so greatly, price ranges rather than set figures are provided. These are coded A through I:

A = $25,000 and over
B = $10,000 to $25,000
C = $5,000 to $10,000
D = $2,500 to $5,000
E = $1,000 to $2,500
F = $500 to $1,000
G = $250 to $500
H = $100 to $250
I = under $100

THE WOMAN'S DAY
Dictionary of
FURNITURE

Beds

An antique bed can be a most appealing object in the bedroom. Properly fitted with modern springs and mattress, it can also be an extremely comfortable everyday item. A bed of almost any sort was a prize possession in the North American colonies until the mid-18th century. The most romantic and popular of old-fashioned beds today is the freestanding canopied four-poster, which came into use in America in the early 1700s. This is a simplified version of the elaborately draped and curtained English Renaissance bedstead which was either freestanding or enclosed within a sleeping alcove. The trend toward simplification in beds continued until the mid-1800s. It was then that the bed, at least that used in the master bedroom, grew heavier and often featured a towering headboard and perhaps even a half-tester overhead. The most commonly used bed, however, remained a low four-post model, such as those illustrated on pp. 16-17. It was during the second half of the 19th century that metal beds also became popular, especially those of curved brass tubing. The preference during the colonial period for a canopied bed that might also be fitted with curtains never quite faded away during the Victorian age. The form enjoyed a new popularity after the Centennial celebration of 1876.

A day bed is exactly as described: a place to recline during daylight hours. Use of such an object gradually faded away in the 1800s as the sofa or couch became a more common household item. Only the chaise longue remains as a reminder of the graceful form.

DAY BEDS

1. American, late 1600s, walnut, carved and caned backrest, seat cushion. **(C)**
2. American, c. 1700, walnut, carved and caned backrest, caned seat. **(D)**
3. French, Louis XV, 1723-74, outward curving scroll ends, seat cushions. **(D)**

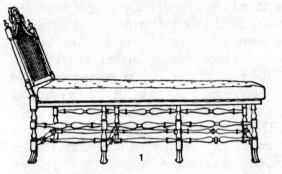

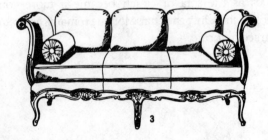

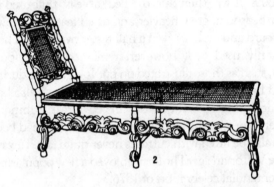

4. American, Queen Anne, early 1700s, seat cushion. **(D)**
5. American, Chippendale, 1760s, country origin, seat cushion. **(D)**
6. French, Louis XVI, 1774-92, painted frame, seat cushions. **(F)**

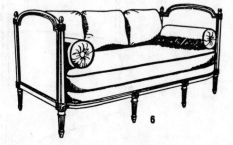

STANDARD BEDS

1. French, Louis XV, 1723-74, carved fruitwood. **(E)**
2. French, Louis XVI, 1774-92, painted frame. **(F)**
3. American, late 1700s, maple, turned and blocked posts, curved headboard, canopy. **(D)**

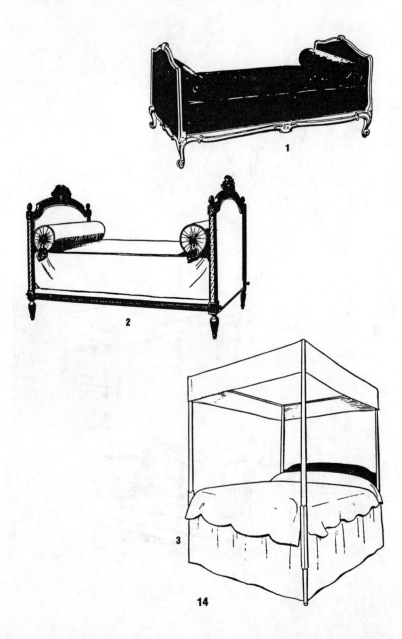

4. American, 1785-1800, field bed, arched tester frame, vase-shaped posts, tapered legs. **(E)**
5. English, 1790-early 1800s, sleigh bed, rosewood, brass appliqués. **(F)**
6. American, 1815-40, crown bed, mahogany, brass appliqués. **(E)**

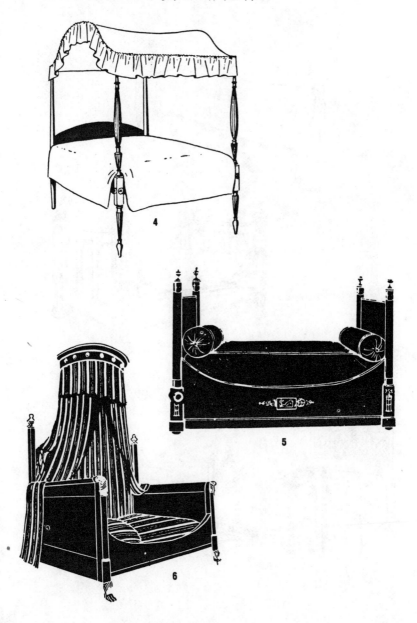

7. American, 19th century, low-post bed, block and turned posts, plain headboard. **(G)**

8. American, 1830s-50s, paneled bed, mahogany, octagonal posts, Gothic arched panels. **(E)**

9. American, 1830s-50s, paneled bed, square posts, Gothic arched panels, half-tester. **(E)**

10. American, 1840s-80s, spool bed, spool-turned posts, spindles, head and footboards. **(E)**

11. American, 1840s-80s, spool bed, spool-turned spindles and rails. **(F)**

12. American, 1850s-60s, by Prudent Mallard, shaped head and footboards, half-tester. **(D)**

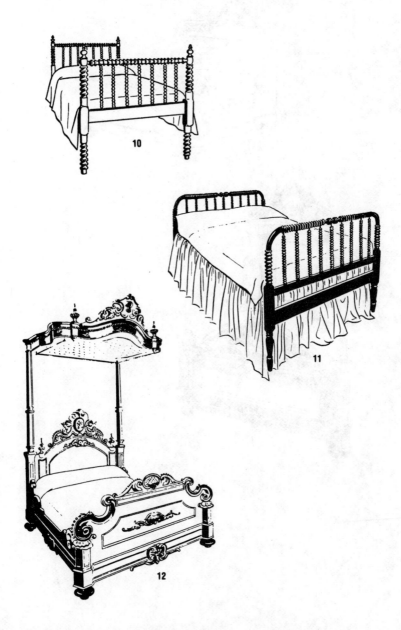

13. American, 1850s-60s, by John Belter, laminated rosewood. **(C)**
14. American, 1870s-80s, paneled head and footboards, applied moldings. **(F)**

13

14

Benches

Benches are such utilitarian objects that they often do not appear in books on antique furniture for the home. Traditionally considered a seat without a back, a bench may be an extraordinarily beautiful piece of furniture if it was formed by a skilled craftsman. Among the most prized objects of this type today are the simply joined and turned benches of the early colonial American period. Equally handsome are the braced-plank and carved-end benches of the 19th-century Shakers. Benches are often used today, as in the past, for seating around a harvest or trestle table or against the wall in an entryway or anteroom where they provide a useful place for resting or changing footgear. Today benches are also used for displaying house plants.

Much more elegant backless forms for seating are the window seats which became popular in England and France in the 18th century. One such simple form, in the French style with outscrolled arms, is illustrated on the following page (no. 2). A second popular form was the neoclassical arched seat (no. 3). Window seats were of course intended to be used in front of a long window which, in the late 1700s and early 1800s, might reach to the floor.

1. American, 17th century, turned legs and feet, plain stretchers. **(F)**
2. English, Hepplewhite, 1780-1800, window seat, mahogany, carved and inlaid. **(F)**
3. English, Regency, early 1800s, carved and gilded. **(F)**
4. American, Shaker, early 1800s, butternut wood with leather-covered seat. **(E)**
5. American, Shaker, early to mid-1800s, pine, braced construction. **(G)**

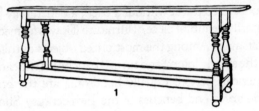

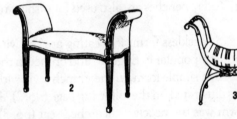

Bookcases

A freestanding bookcase was at first very much of a gentleman's luxury. The use of a special piece of furniture for the storage and display of bound printed material slowly increased in North America during the colonial period and 1800s as books themselves became more commonly available. As prize possessions and a sign of cultivation, books deserved to be openly displayed. Such English cabinetmakers as Chippendale and Hepplewhite designed beautiful cases for bound volumes, and the basic classical forms which they employed were copied throughout the world. The traditional 18th-century English-style bookcase, such as that illustrated on the following page (no. 1), is still very popular today. The bookcase was often built in combination with a secretary or desk, as a convenient place to store record books as well as more literary works. There was another reason for this multi-purpose approach: even by the late 1800s, few families possessed more than several dozen volumes requiring shelving.

Perhaps the most beautiful bookcase form is the breakfront of three sections with a higher and projecting center section. Today, when books are found everywhere, it may seem more appropriate to adorn the shelves of such a magnificent cabinet with china or other valuable objects. Equally impressive, although less monumental, are various types of oak bookcases, some made in combination with desks (p. 23, no. 6), which became popular in the late 1800s. Simple oak cases with glass doors or sliding glass panels were widely manufactured in the early 1900s for use at home and in libraries. These, too, may be put to attractive use today.

1. English, Queen Anne, early 1700s, bureau bookcase, walnut, mirror glass in door fronts. **(C)**
2. English, Chippendale, 1750-90, bureau bookcase, mahogany, scrolled pediment, urn finials. **(C)**
3. English, 1760-1810, by Robert Adam, low-carved festoons and medallions. **(C)**

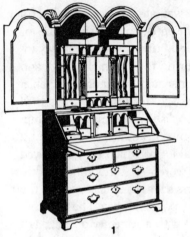

4. French, Louis XVI, 1774-92, bibliotheque, fruitwood, shelves and glass doors. **(D)**

5. English, Sheraton, 1790-1810, bookstand, satinwood and inlays, cupboard base. **(E)**

6. American, late 1800s, secretary bookcase, golden oak, glass door. **(F)**

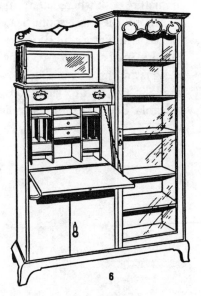

Boxes

THE variety of boxes made in North America for use in the home from the 17th century to the 1900s is almost without number. This most utilitarian of forms can be adapted to many uses. Each of the examples illustrated in the following pages was meant for storage, and each has a portability that allows it to be used in almost any area of the house. Among the major varieties are bible and writing boxes; sewing boxes; spice chests or boxes; wall boxes for candles, pipes, salt, and cutlery; and jewelry, hat, and cosmetic boxes.

The most striking and valuable of these containers are the carved bible and writing boxes which date from the colonial period. As the most important family possession, the bible was traditionally kept in an ornamental case of some sort. The bible box was also a convenient place for safekeeping valuable papers such as deeds, certificates, and wills and testaments. Very similar in style to the bible box is the writing box, a miniature desk where letters and writing supplies were kept.

Among the most sophisticated boxes are spice chests designed as miniature cupboards or cabinets in which to store expensive ingredients for cooking. The most delightful of the designs are the carved Queen Anne and Chippendale pieces made in the mid to late 1700s in New England and Pennsylvania. Several examples are illustrated on p. 26.

BIBLE/WRITING BOXES

1. American, 17th century, geometric chisel carving, molded edges. **(D)**
2. American, early 1700s, also known as desk box, carved and painted. **(E)**
3. American, Hudson Valley, early 1700s, poplar, carved decoration. **(E)**
4. American, c. 1740s, line, volute, and berry inlay. **(E)**
5. American, Pennsylvania-German, late 1700s, paneled and painted. **(E)**
6. American, 19th century, burnished mahogany, stenciled black bands. **(I)**

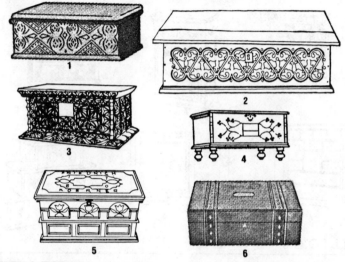

SEWING BOXES

1. American, c. 1790, indented equipment tray, mirror glass in lid. **(F)**
2. American, late 1700s, spool box, mother-of-pearl bound in metal. **(G)**
3. American, c. 1850, thread box, walnut, shallow drawer and cupboards. **(G)**
4. American, 1870-90, walnut, carved and beveled cover. **(I)**

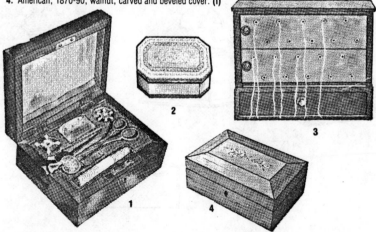

SPICE CHESTS/BOXES

1. American, 17th century, carved, applied molding. **(E)**
2. American, Chester County, Pa., mid-1700s, walnut, herringbone, line and berry inlay. **(F)**
3. American, Chippendale, late 1700s, six-drawer. **(F)**
4. American, Pennsylvania, c. 1725-50, walnut, small drawers. **(E)**
5. American, New England, late 1700s, incised decoration. **(F)**
6. American, Shaker, early 1800s, pine, pyramid of drawers. **(F)**

WALL BOXES

1. American, Pennsylvania-German, early 1700s, pine, for salt. **(F)**
2. American, mid-1700s, walnut, scrolled hanger and inlaid ornaments, for cutlery. **(F)**
3. American, mid-1700s, pine, for long-stemmed clay pipes. **(G)**
4. American, early 1800s, pine, hinged cover and bottom drawer, for candles. **(H)**
5. American, early 1800s, pine, Cupid's bow edge, for candles. **(I)**

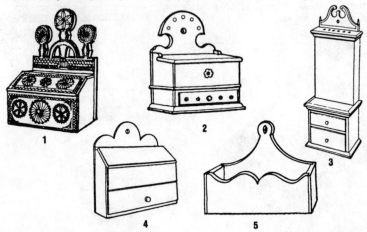

ASSORTED BOXES

1. American, late 1700s, domed lid, painted decoration, for trinkets. **(G)**
2. American, late 1700s, pine, stained red and painted, for storing a tricorn hat. **(E)**
3. American, Hepplewhite, 1780s-early 1800s, mahogany, inlaid and reeded, for knives. **(G)**
4. American, Pennsylvania-German, 1750-1800, cedar, painted, bride box. **(F)**
5. American, Pennsylvania-German, early 1800s, pine, painted decoration, sliding top, for candles. **(F)**
6. American, Shaker, 19th century, overlapping wood strips, splint box. **(I)**
7. American, Shaker, 19th century, nest of splint boxes. **(G)**
8. American, mid-1800s, cherry, with shallow tray, lined with wallpaper, cosmetic box. **(I)**

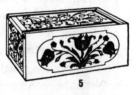

Cabinets

A cabinet is usually a large piece of furniture built for storage or display. Unlike the cupboard, it is rarely a built-in feature of a room. In the 17th century the making of cabinets in England and France was raised to a high art, and craftsmen undertaking these monumental pieces reigned supreme among wood artisans. By the 18th century the term "cabinet-maker" was commonly applied to craftsmen of various types of case furniture. Nearly every great cabinetmaker created magnificent designs employing marquetry, carved and applied ornament, or inlay. Rarely is a piece of furniture termed a cabinet made of such a common wood as pine. Cabinets of the 18th century were usually made of mahogany; in the 1800s the preferred wood was frequently walnut or rosewood.

What might be stored in such a special place? China was intended for the Chinese Chippendale cabinet introduced in England and America in the mid-1700s (see illustration no. 4, on the opposite page); priceless serving dishes or fine liqueurs might have been stored in the highly-carved Victorian Renaissance piece that looks as if it might have been designed by the renowned American designer John H. Belter (p. 30, no. 7).

The only type of cabinet which has survived in popularity in the 20th century is one for china or other curios. It is usually provided with glass-paneled doors and may be securely locked. The design is straightforward, without the embellishments of the Victorian craftsman.

1. French, Provincial, 1700s, fruitwood, rectangular and scrolled panels, cabriole legs. **(E)**
2. English, 1750s-60s, by William Vile, carved and applied ornament, false drawers. **(D)**
3. English, Chippendale, 1750s-90s, kingwood, marquetry decoration. **(E)**
4. American, Chippendale, 1755-80, mahogany, with fretwork, for china. **(D)**

5. American, Sheraton, 1790-1810, mahogany and grained mahogany veneer, glass doors. **(D)**
6. English, Regency, 1795-1820, rosewood, paneled, brass appliqué trim. **(E)**
7. American, 1855-75, rosewood with tulipwood and ebony inlay. **(E)**
8. American, Eastlake, 1870-90, incised design on door, applied molding, corner columns. **(F)**

5

6

7

8

Candlestands

Many different kinds of stands were once used in the American home and these are described and illustrated on pp. 131-33. The candlestand, however, is a unique early form and as such is highly collectible today. While a colonial or early 19th-century household might do without a wash or dressing stand, it was more than likely to be supplied with one or two candlestands in the principal rooms. A relatively small piece of furniture, it is sturdy but portable. In its time it was not difficult to make and usually consisted of only a base and top. The most common antique form, the tripod-base stand, is a simple but elegant object. It serves equally well today as a stand for an electric lamp.

The candlestand derives in form from the Renaissance torchère, illustrated on the following page (no. 1). Most of the designs of the 18th and 19th centuries employ a similar tripod base, and these include pieces as diverse as those made by the American Shakers (no. 10) and by early 19th-century French craftsmen (no. 9).

The most unusual and rare candlestands are the primitive devices which incorporate a holder in the stand. One such object, with a rachet device to adjust the height of two candles, is shown in illustration no. 4. It is a precursor of the modern adjustable bridge lamp.

1. French, late 1600s, tripod base, gilded. **(G)**
2. English, 1720-60, walnut, tripod base and octagonal top. **(F)**
3. English, Chippendale, 1755-60, mahogany, fretwork support and gallery. **(G)**
4. American, 18th century, maple, adjustable bar for two candles. **(F)**
5. American, Hepplewhite, 1780-1800, urn pedestal. **(F)**
6. American, Federal, 1785-1815, tripod base, baluster shaft. **(F)**
7. American, Sheraton, 1790-1810, tilt top. **(F)**
8. French, Directoire, 1795-1804, for a plant or candle. **(G)**
9. French, Empire, 1804-14, griffin-carved legs. **(G)**
10. American, Shaker, 19th century, drawer, turned shaft, and rod feet. **(F)**

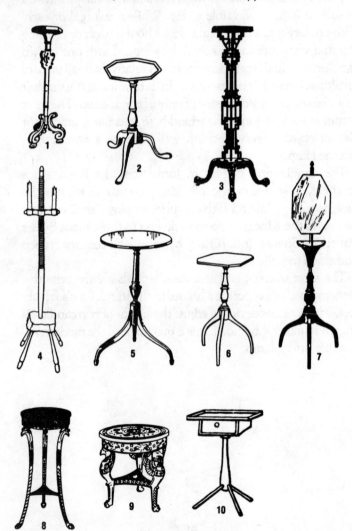

Card Tables

TABLES constructed especially for gaming and gambling began to appear in the late 16th century. Needlework "boards" attached to the tabletop provided the patterns needed for various games, which included such gentlemanly pastimes as cards, chess, dice, and backgammon. As time went on, the tables became ever more elaborate and specialized: many included such features as "guinea holes," counter saucers, and corners made to hold candlesticks. Card tables reached the height of their popularity in 18th-century England and were considered an indispensable item in upper-class households. The English passion for gaming tables was transported to America with the colonists: numerous exquisite examples of these specialized pieces exist in a variety of 18th- and 19th-century styles ranging from Queen Anne to Hepplewhite to Empire.

The precursors of today's practical, collapsible card tables, early gaming tables are usually made with folding tops. Common among both English and American tables is a two-leaved top hinged in the middle and with a swinging leg below to provide support when the table is opened. Often the open table is covered with baize which provides a soft, relatively undamageable surface and helps to muffle the clatter of rolling dice. Most popular in England and America, card tables were also produced in France and Italy and elsewhere on the Continent. Two examples illustrated on p. 37 (nos. 1, 2) show nonfolding French gaming tables; one has a reversible top, making it possible to use the same table for two "board" games.

AMERICAN

1. Queen Anne, 1725-50, needlework top, oval counter saucers, corners for candlesticks. **(C)**
2. Chippendale, 1750-75, oval counter saucers, corners for candlesticks, fifth leg support. **(C)**
3. Hepplewhite, 1780-1800, mahogany with light-colored inlay. **(E)**
4. Hepplewhite, Baltimore, 1780-1800, mahogany with eagle inlays. **(D)**
5. Hepplewhite, New York City, 1780-1815, by John Hewitt, fold-over top. **(D)**
6. Hepplewhite, 1780-1800, straight tapered inlaid legs, fold-over top. **(E)**

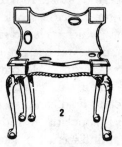

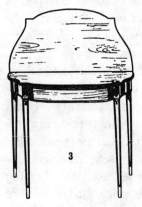

7. Hepplewhite, 1780-1800, inlay stringing and medallions, fold-over top. **(E)**
8. Hepplewhite, 1790s, by Elbert Anderson, fold-over top. **(D)**
9. Sheraton, Philadelphia, 1790-1815, carving. **(E)**
10. Sheraton, 1790-1815, serpentine skirt and fold-over top, inlaid corner blocks. **(E)**
11. Empire, Baltimore, 1790-1815, mahogany, bellflower and medallion inlays. **(E)**
12. Duncan Phyfe, 1792-1815, octagon skirt and hinged and pivoted top, lyre pedestal. **(E)**

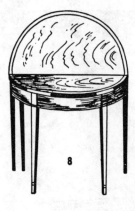

13. Duncan Phyfe, 1792-1815, serpentine skirt and fold-over top, acanthus carving. **(E)**
14. Duncan Phyfe, 1800-15, spread-eagle support, leaf-carved legs. **(E)**
15. Federal, c. 1800, by Samuel McIntire, mahogany, carved mount. **(C)**
16. Empire, 1805-15, by Charles Honoré Lannuier, rosewood, gilded mounts. **(C)**
17. Sheraton, c. 1810, five reeded legs, fold-over top, serpentine skirt. **(E)**
18. Empire, 1800-20, canted corners, lyre support, winged paw feet. **(D)**

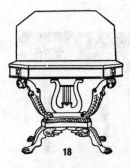

ENGLISH

1. Queen Anne, 1700-20, walnut, fold-over top, cabriole legs. **(D)**
2. Queen Anne, 1700-20, mahogany, fold-over top, candlestick corners. **(D)**
3. Early Georgian, 1720-60, fold-over top, richly carved cabriole legs. **(D)**
4. Hepplewhite, 1780-1800, mahogany, bellflower and leaf inlay. **(E)**

FRENCH

1. Louis XV, Provincial, 1723-74, gaming table. **(E)**
2. Louis XVI, 1774-92, backgammon table, reversible top. **(E)**

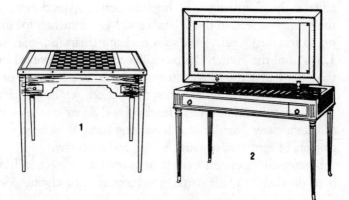

CHAIRS

IT is thought that chairs were first used by the Egyptians in the second and third centuries before Christ; the practice of sitting on a portable seat with legs, arms, and/or backs was also common in both ancient Greece and Rome. Later the chair almost disappeared, and there is little evidence that it was used in the Middle Ages by anyone except members of the nobility. During the Renaissance, the Italians revived the custom of sitting in chairs; and these pieces of furniture were often treated as objects worthy of ornamentation. By the end of the 17th century, chairs were common in Europe and America; chairs for the upper classes were made by skilled craftsmen in a plethora of designs and styles and were often padded, cushioned, and upholstered; simpler constructions were available to the middle and lower classes. Seventeenth-century chairmakers in France were among the first to concentrate on the formation of elegant and extremely comfortable designs. From the period of Louis XIV to the Empire, the French produced innumerable variations on the form: from the rectangular Louis XIV armchairs (p. 48, nos. 2, 3), to the "easy" chairs of the Régence (p. 49, nos. 1, 3), to the delicate becushioned creations of the Louis XVI period (p. 50, nos. 1-5) the styles developed by French artisans influenced craftsmen all over the Continent. The English created styles distinctly their own—as seen in the William and Mary armchair (p. 46, no. 2) and the Queen Anne splat-back armchairs (p., 46, nos. 1, 2)—until the French Rococo influence began to prevail in the latter half of the 18th century. Despite the taste for the ornate which predominated during that period, Windsor chairs came into use at that time in England and America; they are still immensely popular and have long been considered exemplars of lightness, comfort, shape, and economy.

Because chairs appear in so many varieties, this section has been divided into four parts: armchairs, rocking chairs, side chairs, and wing chairs.

Armchairs

American

PILGRIM CENTURY, 1600s

1. Spindle chair, three-legged, triangular seat and stretcher. **(B)**
2. Child's chair, maple and elm, simple turnings. **(B)**
3. Brewster-type armchair, two-tier spindles. **(B)**
4. Wainscot armchair, white oak, carved paneling. **(B)**
5. Bannister-back armchair, carved crest, scrolled arms, Spanish feet. **(C)**
6. Slat-back armchair, shaped slat, heavy posts, rush seat. **(C)**
7. Carver-type armchair, tier of spindles, turned posts, rush seat. **(C)**

1

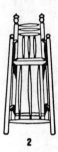

2

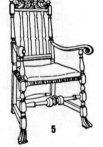

3

4

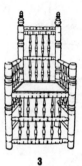

5

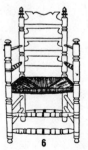

6

7

EARLY 18TH-CENTURY AND QUEEN ANNE, 1725-50

1. Wainscot armchair, Chester County, Pa., walnut. **(B)**
2. Wainscot armchair, paneled frame, square posts. **(C)**
3. Turned armchair, Virginia, cherry posts and back, hickory stretchers. **(C)**
4. Banister-back armchair, maple, rush seat. **(E)**
5. Slat-back armchair, painted. **(E)**
6. Queen Anne armchair, hoop-shaped back, solid vase-shaped splat, shell carving. **(E)**
7. Queeen Anne armchair, Hudson Valley, fiddle-back, rush seat. **(F)**
8. Settle chair, high back, wide wings, chest seat. **(F)**

1

3

4

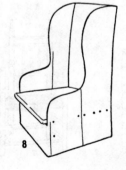
5

6

7

8

CHIPPENDALE, 1755-80

1. Rectangular-back armchair, Cupid's-bow crest rail, shell carving. **(D)**
2. Armchair, carved mahogany, tapestry covering. **(E)**

HEPPLEWHITE, 1780-1800

1. Shield-shaped-back armchair, upholstered seat. **(E)**
2. Shield-shaped-back armchair, mahogany frame, upholstered seat. **(E)**
3. Shield-shaped-back armchair, carved frame, upholstered back and seat. **(E)**
4. Oval-shaped-back armchair, Prince of Wales feathers carved in back, upholstered seat. **(E)**
5. Columnar-back armchair, pierced splats, upholstered seat. **(F)**

SHERATON, 1790-1810

1. Martha Washington-style armchair; Salem, Mass.; upholstered seat and back. **(D)**
2. Carved-splat armchair, reeded legs, spade feet, upholstered seat. **(F)**
3. Columnar-back armchair, New York City, upholstered seat. **(F)**
4. Columnar-back armchair with crest rail, mahogany, upholstered seat. **(F)**
5. Columnar-back armchair, New York City, upholstered seat. **(F)**

DUNCAN PHYFE, 1792-1815

1. Curule-form armchair, rounded cane seat, dog's-paw front feet. **(F)**
2. Curule-form armchair, mahogany, rounded upholstered seat, brass paw feet. **(F)**

EMPIRE, 1815-40

1. Scrolled-arm or Grecian armchair, upholstered back panel, crest rail. **(F)**
2. Elbow armchair, mahogany, scrolled back and arms, turned legs, upholstered back and seat. **(F)**
3. Reclining chair, mahogany, adjustable back and footrest, upholstered in velvet. **(E)**

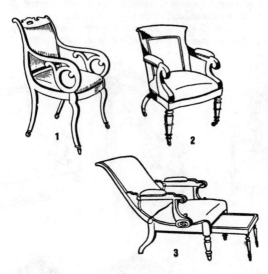

VICTORIAN, 1840-1900

1, 2. Husband-wife armchairs, balloon back (oval frames), upholstered seats and backs. **(pr., E)**
3. Elizabethan armchair, spool-turned, walnut, high back, upholstered seat and back. **(F)**

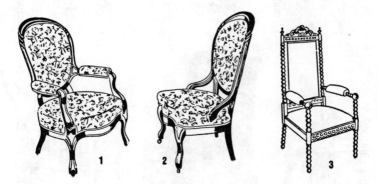

4. Renaissance Revival gentleman's armchair, rosewood, upholstered seat and back. **(E)**
5. Renaissance Revival armchair, by John Belter, laminated rosewood, upholstered seat and back. **(E)**
6. Victorian Cottage armchair, walnut; spool-turned legs, uprights, and spindles. **(G)**
7. Renaissance Revival armchair, mahogany with inlay, oval frame back. **(F)**
8. Curule armchair, walnut, crested and upholstered back, upholstered seat and armrests. **(G)**
9. Renaissance Revival armchair, walnut; deep upholstered back, arm rests, and seat. **(G)**
10. Eastlake armchair, black walnut, upholstered seat and back panel. **(G)**
11. Turkish-style armchair, ebonized wood, upholstered seat and headrest with thick fringe. **(H)**
12. Morris armchair, golden oak, adjustable back, tufted seat and back cushions. **(G)**

WINDSOR, 1750-1815

1. Bow-back baby's highchair with footrest, H-stretcher. **(F)**
2. Bow-back armchair, New Jersey, with writing arm, H-stretcher. **(F)**
3. Bow-back armchair, knuckle-carved arm ends, H-stretcher. **(E)**
4. Arch-back armchair, New York, braced back, H-stretcher. **(F)**
5. Low-back armchair, Philadelphia, out-scrolled arms, H-stretcher. **(E)**
6. Fan-back armchair with writing arm, New England, H-stretcher. **(E)**
7. Comb-back armchair with writing arm and drawer, cut-back saddle seat, plain crest, H-stretcher. **(F)**
8. Arch-back armchair with comb, braced back, H-stretcher. **(D)**
9. Low-back armchair with comb, spiral-carved ears, H-stretcher. **(D)**

English

17TH CENTURY

1. Wainscot armchair, paneled oak, gouge or chisel carving. **(C)**
2. William and Mary armchair, walnut, serpentine X-stretcher, upholstered seat and back. **(C)**

QUEEN ANNE, 1700-20, AND EARLY GEORGIAN, 1720-60

1. Queen Anne corner or roundabout chair, splat back, X-stretcher, upholstered seat. **(D)**
2. Queen Anne armchair, walnut frame, fiddle-shaped splat, upholstered seat, H-stretcher. **(E)**
3. Early-Georgian armchair, gilt decoration, carved legs and arm supports, velvet upholstery. **(D)**
4. Early-Georgian armchair, carved front cabriole legs; upholstered back, seat, and arm supports. **(D)**
5. Early-Georgian armchair, walnut, carved front cabriole legs, upholstered seat, splat back. **(E)**
6. Early-Georgian armchair, mahogany, latticework back, upholstered seat. **(D)**

CHIPPENDALE, 1760-80

1. Armchair, by Ince and Mayhew, carved and gilded; upholstered seat, back, and arm supports. **(C)**
2. Corner chair, interlaced scroll splat back, upholstered seat, X-stretcher. **(D)**
3. Lyre-back armchair, mahogany, upholstered seat, carved frame. **(E)**
4. Armchair, by John Cobb, carved pierced splat back. **(D)**

ROBERT ADAM, 1760-80

1. Oval-shaped-back armchair, carved and gilded frame, French style, upholstered. **(E)**
2. Armchair, beechwood, upholstered seat, back, and arms. **(D)**
3. Oval-shaped-back armchair, carved and fluted frame, French style, satin upholstery. **(E)**

HEPPLEWHITE, 1780-1800

1. Shield-back armchair, beechwood frame, upholstered seat, receding arm supports. **(E)**
2. Shield-back armchair, tapered legs, receding arm supports, upholstered seat. **(E)**

WINDSOR, 18TH CENTURY

1. Arch-back armchair with comb and splat, elm or yew, cabriole front legs, H-stretcher. **(F)**
2. Bow-back armchair, elm or yew, back with openwork splat. **(G)**
3. Low-back armchair, back with openwork splat, cabriole front legs, H-stretcher. **(F)**

French

LOUIS XIV, 1643-1715

1. Armchair, caned seat and back, serpentine-cross stretcher. **(E)**
2. Armchair, upholstered back and seat, H-stretcher. **(E)**
3. Armchair, upholstered seat and back, serpentine-cross stretcher. **(E)**

RÉGENCE, 1715-23

1. Armchair, closed arms, carved frame. **(F)**
2. Armchair, beechwood, caned seat and back, X-stretcher. **(F)**
3. Armchair, carved beechwood, cabriole legs, X-stretcher. **(F)**

LOUIS XV, 1723-74

1. Bannister-back armchair, beechwood, rush seat, H-stretcher. **(F)**
2. Armchair, upholstered back and seat, cabriole legs. **(F)**
3. Desk armchair, upholstered, cabriole legs. **(F)**
4. Corner chair, walnut, leather-upholstered seat and back, cabriole legs. **(F)**
5. Armchair, walnut; tapestry-upholstered seat, arm supports, and back; cabriole legs. **(F)**
6. Armchair, caned back, upholstered seat, cabriole legs. **(F)**

7. Armchair; upholstered back, seat, and arm supports; carved and painted frame, cabriole legs. **(F)**

8. Desk chair, caned back and seat, cabriole legs. **(F)**

LOUIS XVI, 1774-92

1. Armchair; upholstered seat, arm supports, and back; tapered legs. **(E)**

2. Armchair; upholstered seat, arm supports, and back; tapered legs. **(E)**

3. Low armchair, upholstered frame and seat cushion, carved and gilded frame, tapered legs. **(E)**

4. Armchair; upholstered seat, back, and arm supports; carved and gilded frame, fluted legs. **(F)**

5. Oval-back armchair, walnut; tapestry-upholstered seat, back, and arm supports; tapered legs. **(F)**

EMPIRE, 1804-14

1. Desk chair, ormolu mounts, upholstered, paw feet. **(F)**
2. Armchair, carved swan-neck arm supports, upholstered. **(F)**
3. Armchair, rosewood, swan-neck arm supports, saber legs. **(F)**

Rocking Chairs

NEW ENGLAND AND PENNSYLVANIA, 18TH AND EARLY 19TH CENTURIES

1. Comb-back rocker, Pennsylvania, arrow splats. **(F)**
2. High-back rocker, New England, arched slats. **(F)**
3. Boston rocker, New England, saddle seat, gilt stenciled decoration. **(F)**
4. Wagon-seat twin rocker, New England, hickory, rush seats, double stretcher. **(E)**

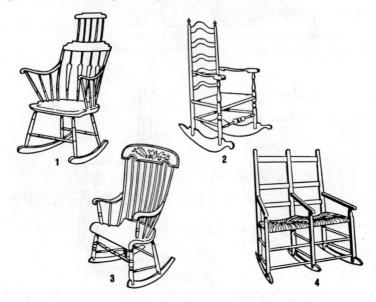

VICTORIAN, 1840-80

1. Lady rocker, oval-shaped back, finger-molded frame, upholstered seat and back. **(G)**
2. Contour rocker-chair, painted iron frame, velvet upholstery. **(G)**
3. Bentwood rocker, laminated birchwood frame, cane seat and back. **(F)**
4. Folding rocker, maple frame, beech rockers, upholstered seat and back. **(G)**

SHAKER, 19TH CENTURY

1. Armless rocker, used for sewing, maple frame, rush seat. **(G)**
2. Slat-back rocker, maple frame, woven-tape seat, finials on back posts. **(F)**

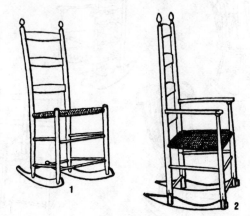

Side Chairs

American

PILGRIM CENTURY, 1600s

1. Side chair, seat and back covered in Turkey-work upholstery. **(C)**
2. Slat-back side chair, rush seat; turned posts, legs, and stretchers. **(D)**
3. Carver-type side chair, spindle back, turned top rail and stretchers. **(D)**

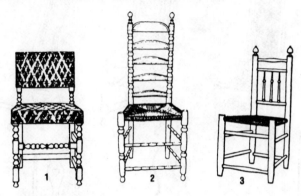

EARLY 18TH CENTURY

1. Side chair, walnut, painted black, leather upholstery. **(E)**
2. William and Mary slipper chair; turned posts, front legs, and stretcher; leather upholstery. **(E)**
3. William and Mary side chair, bannister back, carved crest, Spanish front feet. **(F)**

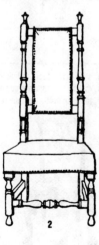

4. William and Mary high-back chair, caned panel and seat, carved Flemish-scroll feet. **(E)**

5. William and Mary side chair, carved and turned maple frame, leather upholstery. **(E)**

6. William and Mary spoon-back side chair, wood graining, upholstered. **(E)**

7. Slat-back side chair, New Jersey, maple, turned seat rails, rush seat. **(F)**

8. Moravian plank side chair, walnut, carved back with cut-outs. **(F)**

9. Pierced splat-back side chair, Hudson Valley, rush seat. **(F)**

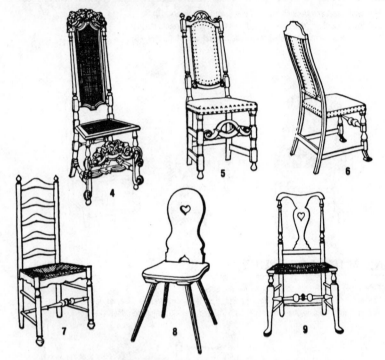

CHIPPENDALE, 1755-80

1. Scroll splat-back side chair, Philadelphia, shell in crest rail, upholstered seat. **(E)**

2. Scroll splat-back side chair, Philadelphia, mahogany, upholstered seat. **(E)**

3. Scroll splat-back side chair, Philadelphia, tassel in splat, shell in crest rail, upholstered seat. **(E)**

HEPPLEWHITE, 1780-1800

1. Side chair, mahogany, vase-shaped splat, molded back uprights, upholstered seat. **(F)**
2. Side chair; Newport, R.I.; urn and bellflower carving, vase-shaped splat, upholstered seat. **(E)**
3. Shield-back side chair, mahogany, medallion in back, upholstered seat. **(E)**
4. Shield-back side chair, mahogany, urn carving in back, upholstered seat. **(E)**
5. Side chair, vase-shaped splat, urn and drapery carving in back, upholstered seat. **(F)**
6. Shield-back side chair, mahogany, urn and drapery carving in back, upholstered seat. **(E)**
7. Heart-back side chair, serpentine seat, spade feet, upholstered seat. **(F)**
8. Shield-back side chair, by Benjamin Frothingham, Samuel McIntire carver, urn and drapery carving. **(C)**
9. Heart-back side chair, Baltimore, bellflower inlay, upholstered seat. **(E)**

10. Shield-back side chair, Maryland, mahogany, urn and drapery carving, upholstered seat. **(E)**

11. Shield-back side chair, urn and drapery carving, upholstered seat. **(E)**

SHERATON, 1790-1810

1. Carved-splat armchair, Philadelphia, upholstered seat. **(F)**

2. Carved square-back columnar armchair, mahogany, upholstered seat. **(F)**

3. Scroll-back klismos-type side chair, carved slat, paw front feet, upholstered seat. **(G)**

4. Scroll-back klismos-type side chair, eagle-carved center slat, saber legs, upholstered seat. **(G)**

5. Side chair, Philadelphia, carved crest and rail, saber legs, upholstered seat. **(G)**

6. Carved square-back columnar armchair, crested back, pierced splats, upholstered seat. **(G)**

DUNCAN PHYFE, 1792-1815

1. Curule-form-back sidechair, drapery-carved crest, upholstered curved seat, reeded legs. **(F)**
2. Lyre-back side chair, mahogany, carving on front legs, upholstered seat. **(F)**

EARLY 19TH CENTURY

1. Gothic side chair, rosewood, flat cabriole front legs, upholstered seat. **(F)**
2. Splat-back armchair, crest rail with carving, continuous stile and rail, saber legs. **(F)**
3. Gothic side chair, oak, carved back with finials, square legs, wood seat. **(F)**
4. Hitchcock-style side chair, New Jersey, painted, stenciled eagle splat, cane seat. **(F)**
5. Swan-splat side chair, Hudson Valley, painted, cane seat. **(F)**
6. Arrow-back side chair, painted and stenciled, wood seat. **(G)**

7. Arrow-back side chair, painted and stenciled, wood seat. **(G)**
8. Hitchcock-style side chair, eagle cut-out slat, stenciled, cane seat. **(F)**
9. Gothic side chair, rosewood, open quatrefoil under finial, upholstered back and seat. **(F)**

VICTORIAN, 1840-1900

1. Hitchcock side chair, painted black and stenciled, cane seat. **(G)**
2. Louis XV-style chair, walnut, cartouche back, velour upholstery. **(F)**
3. Rococo side chair, black walnut, carved crest rail, upholstered seat. **(G)**
4. Rococo side chair, carved and painted back, upholstered seat, cabriole legs. **(F)**
5. Rococo side chair, walnut, carved crest, upholstered seat. **(G)**
6. Rococo side chair, by John Belter, laminated rosewood, grape and scroll carving **(D)**

7. Renaissance side chair, scroll-carved uprights, upholstered seat and back. **(G)**
8. Renaissance side chair, high back with carved interlaced splat, upholstered seat. **(F)**
9. Reclining side chair, cast and wrought iron, upholstered, crown-shaped base. **(G)**
10. Eastlake side chair, ebonized frame, flower inlay, upholstered seat. **(G)**
11. Mission side chair, oak frame, square rush seat. **(G)**
12. Cottage side chair, maple frame, bamboo turnings, upholstered seat. **(G)**
13. Rococo side chair, lacquered and inlaid back, caned seat. **(F)**

SHAKER, 19TH CENTURY

1. Shop or counter chair, slat back, finials, woven-tape seat. **(G)**
2. Swivel or revolving chair, wooden seat may be raised or lowered. **(G)**
3. Dining chair, maple, low back, tape seat. **(G)**
4. Tilting side chair, maple, back legs fitted with sockets for tilting backward, tape seat. **(G)**

WINDSOR, 1750-1815

1. Bow-back side chair, braced back, saddle seat, H-stretcher. **(G)**
2. Comb-back side chair, cresting rail with scrolled ears, saddle seat, H-stretcher. **(F)**
3. Double-rail-back side chair, two spindle types, saddle seat. **(G)**

English

QUEEN ANNE, 1700-20

1. Splat-back arm chair, pad feet, upholstered seat. **(F)**
2. Splat-back arm chair, walnut, fiddle-shaped splat, cabriole legs, upholstered seat. **(F)**
3. Splat-back arm chair, carved splat and crest, carved cabriole legs, upholstered seat. **(F)**
4. Reading or straddle chair, mahogany, leather back and seat. **(E)**

CHIPPENDALE, MID-GEORGIAN, 1760-80

1. Ribbon-back side chair, upholstered seat, cabriole legs. **(F)**
2. Vase splat-back chair, mahogany, carved crest and splat, leather seat. **(F)**
3. Ladder-back side chair, straight front legs, upholstered seat. **(G)**
4. Wheel-back side chair, serpentine upholstered seat, tapered legs. **(F)**

ROBERT ADAM, 1765-95

1. Lyre-back side chair, carved splat and crest, tapered legs, upholstered seat. **(D)**

SHERATON, 1790-1810

1. Trellis-back side chair, mahogany, turned feet, upholstered seat. **(G)**
2. Draped fancy side chair, carved and painted wood frame, upholstered seat. **(F)**

French

LOUIS XV, 1723-74

1. Side chair, cabriole legs, carving on crest, upholstered seat and back. **(F)**
2. Side chair, cabriole legs, carving on crest, caned seat and back. **(F)**
3. Ladder-back side chair, beechwood, rush seat. **(F)**

LOUIS XVI, 1774-92

1. Side chair, square back, carved and silvered, velvet-upholstered seat and back. **(F)**
2. Side chair, square back, upholstered seat and back, tapered legs. **(F)**

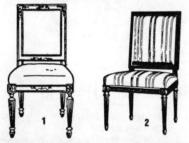

DIRECTOIRE, 1795-1804; EMPIRE, 1804-14

1. Greek-style side chair, shaped and carved back, saber legs, upholstered seat. **(G)**
2. Scroll-back klismos-type side chair, saber legs, upholstered seat. **(G)**
3. Curved-back side chair, carved, upholstered seat, tapered legs. **(G)**
4. Lyre-back side chair, painted, rounded front, tapered and fluted legs. **(G)**

Wing Chairs

1. American, William and Mary, 1690-1725, sharply scrolled arms, cushion, H-stretcher. **(C)**
2. American, William and Mary, 1690-1725, upholstered seat and back, turned legs, H-stretcher. **(C)**
3. French, Louis XV, 1723-74; upholstered seat, back, and cushion; cabriole legs, H-stretcher. **(D)**
4. English, Queen Anne, 1700-20; upholstered back, seat, and cushion; walnut cabriole legs. **(D)**
5. American, Queen Anne, 1725-50, walnut; upholstered seat and back, cabriole legs. **(D)**
6. American, Queen Anne, 1725-50, walnut; upholstered seat, back, and cushion; H-stretcher. **(D)**
7. American, Queen Anne, 1725-50; upholstered seat, back, and cushion; cabriole legs, H-stretcher. **(D)**
8. American, Chippendale, 1755-80, elaborately carved cabriole legs, scrolled arms. **(E)**
9. American, Hepplewhite, 1780-1800, scrolled arms, flaring wings, straight stretchers. **(E)**

1
2
3

4
5
6

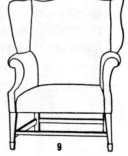

7
8
9

Chests

During medieval times the simple chest was unquestionably the most important piece of furniture in any household, no matter its size or economic status. Used primarily for storage of goods and clothing, as is true today, the chest often did extra duty as a seat, bed, or table, and became a primitive—and rather unwieldy—suitcase when travel plans dictated. While a variety of sophisticated designs and names characterized 18th- and 19th-century French, English, and American chests, their basic, utilitarian function remained. Some, such as the elaborate commodes popular in both Europe and America during the 18th and 19th centuries, combined drawers with hinged doors. The commode, often topped with marble, was used in the salon and dining room to display prize china and silver, and in the bedchamber to store clothing. Gaily-decorated dower chests were especially prized in Pennsylvania-German homes during the late 1700s (see p. 70); more restrained blanket chests, such as the simple Shaker design pictured on the same page, often stood at the foot of the bed, giving easy access to extra or off-season coverings. Such chests often incorporated a drawer or two for additional storage of smaller items.

Bureaus intended for use in the bedchamber often included attached mirrors or dressing glasses. Some, such as the Hepplewhite design pictured on p. 65 (no. 6), were fairly simple in appearance. But in others, such as the elaborately-detailed rosewood dresser on p. 67 (no. 16), the mirror became a more important design element.

American

BUREAUS AND CHESTS OF DRAWERS

1. Guilford chest of drawers, 1700-20, Connecticut, oak, floral and armorial painting. **(C)**
2. Taunton chest of drawers, 1720-50, Massachusetts, pine, scrolled painting of flowers and birds. **(C)**
3. Bureau, Chippendale, 1755-80, mahogany, receding center panel, brass hardware. **(D)**
4. Block-front bureau, Chippendale, 1755-80, Newport, mahogany, brass hardware. **(D)**
5. High chest of drawers, Pennsylvania-German, 1770, walnut, brass hardware. **(C)**
6. Bureau with oval dressing glass, Hepplewhite, 1780-1800, straight front, brass hardware. **(E)**

7. Bow-front bureau, Hepplewhite, 1780-1800, New England, curly maple, brass hardware. **(E)**
8. Bureau with oval dressing glass, Hepplewhite, 1780-1815, New England, mahogany and satinwood. **(E)**
9. Bureau with attached mirror, Sheraton, 1800-20, bowed-chest top, baluster-turned legs. **(E)**
10. Chest of drawers, late 18th century, New England, knobs. **(F)**
11. Chest of drawers, Sheraton, 1800-15, bowed front, reeded and ring-turned corner posts. **(E)**
12. Chest of drawers, Sheraton, 1800-15, bowed front, checkered inlaid banding, flared feet. **(E)**

7

8

9

10

11

12

13. Chest of drawers, late Empire, 1810-20, overhanging top drawer, corner columns. **(F)**
14. Chest of drawers, Pennsylvania-German, 1830-40, Mahantango Valley, painted. **(D)**
15. Counter chest, Shaker, early 19th century, wooden drawer pulls. **(E)**
16. Bureau or dresser with attached arched mirror, 1850-60, by John Belter, rosewood. **(D)**

CHESTS, CHESTS ON CHESTS, CHESTS ON FRAMES

1. Connecticut sunflower chest, late 17th century, sunflower and tulip carving. **(B)**
2. Connecticut sunflower chest, 1670-1725, carved and painted panels. **(B)**

3. Connecticut sunflower chest, 1670-1725, tulip and oak, tulip and sunflower panels. **(B)**
4. Chest, 17th century, oak, cruciform panels in center, lid, two drawers. **(C)**
5. Chest on frame, William and Mary, 1690-1725, lid, single drawer at base. **(E)**
6. Hadley chest, 1700-20, Massachusetts, carved oak, lid, one drawer. **(B)**
7. Guilford chest, 1700-20, Connecticut, pine, painted decoration. **(C)**
8. Taunton chest, 1720-40, Massachusetts, pine, stylized painting of flowers. **(C)**

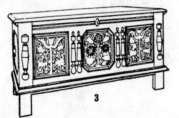

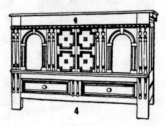

9. Chest-on-frame, Queen Anne, 1725-50, applied bosses, sausage-turned stretchers. **(D)**
10. Chest-on-frame, Queen Anne, 1720-50, molded top, S-curved stretcher, turnip feet. **(D)**
11. Chest-on-chest, Chippendale, 1755-80, New England, carved shell, bonnet top, finials. **(B)**
12. Dower chest, Pennsylvania-German, c. 1780, painted decoration with unicorns. **(C)**
13. Dower chest, Pennsylvania-German, 1780-1800, inscribed name in heart, painted. **(C)**
14. Dower chest, Pennsylvania-German, 1780-1800, poplar, flower-painted arched panels. **(D)**

9

10

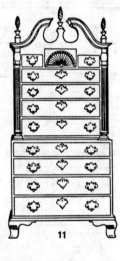

11

12

13

14

15. Dower chest, 1760-1800, Maryland, painted in pastel colors, drawers below. **(D)**
16. Blanket chest, 1750-1800, Virginia, walnut, pinwheel and semicircular inlay. **(E)**
17. Dower chest, early 1800s, Pennsylvania, walnut, inlay in light woods. **(D)**
18. Dower chest, Pennsylvania-German, c. 1800, painted tulips and birds. **(E)**
19. Cordial chest, Hepplewhite, 1780-1800, two drawers flanking cupboard. **(E)**
20. Blanket chest, late 1700s, New England, oak with pine lid, paneled, one drawer in base. **(E)**
21. Blanket chest, Shaker, early 1800s, pine, painted red, one drawer in base. **(E)**

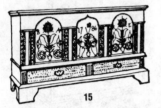

15

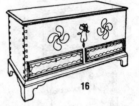

16

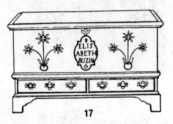

17

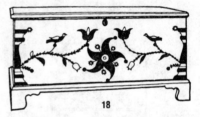

18

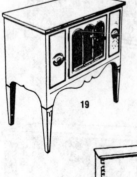

19

20

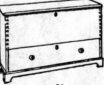

21

COMMODES

1. Chippendale, 1755-80, fretwork gallery, japanned in black and gold. **(C)**
2. Victorian Rococo, 1840-60, by Prudent Mallard, marble top, shelves across back. **(D)**
3. Victorian Cottage, 1850-80, maple, white marble top, carved drawer pulls. **(F)**
4. Victorian Renaissance, 1855-75, black walnut, applied panel, mushroom-turned knobs. **(F)**
5. Eastlake, 1870-1900, walnut with burl veneer panels, marble top, brass drawer pulls. **(F)**

English

CHESTS OF DRAWERS, AND CHESTS ON CHESTS

1. Chest of drawers, William and Mary, 1690-1700, walnut with oyster inlay, large ball feet. **(D)**
2. Chest-on-chest, early Georgian, 1715-50, broken pediment top, fluted columns. **(C)**
3. Chest of drawers, Chippendale, 1750-90, Rococo shape and carving, French scroll feet. **(D)**
4. Chest of drawers, mid-Georgian, c. 1765, mahogany, gilt-bronze hoof feet. **(D)**
5. Chest of drawers, Hepplewhite, 1780-1800, mahogany, serpentine, inlay and pressbanding. **(D)**

1

3

4

5

2

COMMODES

1. Mid-Georgian, 1760-1810, marquetry and inlay, gilt brass mounts, bow-front. **(B)**
2. Chippendale, 1770-90, mahogany, inlay, bow front. **(B)**
3. Sheraton, c. 1795, harewood and satinwood, inlaid, painted. **(D)**

French

COMMODES

1. Régence, 1715-23, walnut, ornamental moldings.**(B)**
2. Régence, 1715-23, walnut, serpentine drawers, ornamental moldings. **(B)**

3. Louis XV, 1723-74, chiffonier, drawer for each day of the week. **(C)**
4. Louis XV, 1723-74, commode à vantaux, oak, surface carving. **(C)**
5. Louis XV, 1723-74, two-drawer, marble top, marquetry decoration. **(C)**
6. Louis XV, 1723-74, two-drawer, bronze doré trim. **(C)**
7. Louis XV, 1723-74, en tombeaux, three-drawer, short legs. **(C)**
8. Louis XVI, 1774-92, mahogany, marble top, fluted posts. **(D)**

9. Louis XVI, 1774-92, tulipwood, marble top, fluted posts, bronze doré trim. **(D)**

10. Louis XVI, 1774-92, marble top, inlaid drawers. **(D)**

11. Louis XVI, 1774-92, demilune shape, three-drawer and open shelves. **(D)**

12. Louis XVI, 1774-92, demilune shape, two-drawer, side cabinets, marble top. **(D)**

13. Directoire, 1795-1804, mahogany, marble top, rich marquetry. **(D)**

14. Empire, 1804-14, mahogany, three-drawer, overhanging top, columnar corner posts. **(E)**

Clocks

INITIALLY encased in brass or other metals, clock mechanisms were not placed in crafted wooden cases until the late 17th century. During the reign of Louis XIV (1643-1715), the first wooden cases for tall case or grandfather clocks were designed to hold the pendulum and weights necessary for the popular mechanical timekeeper perfected in England by William Clement. Elaborate and showy, French clock cases, whether tall case (p. 78, no. 1), shelf or mantel (p. 77, nos. 1 and 2), or wall (p. 80, no. 1) are often intricately carved and embellished with gilded bronze, marble, ebony, or other valuable substances. English and American clock cases of the 18th century are somewhat less ostentatious, though no less beautiful. Clock cases, of course, are "furniture" to house the works of the timekeeper and, as such, clearly reflect the changing tastes and styles of the household furniture that clock cases were designed to complement. It is hardly surprising, then, to find clock cases in all the prevailing popular furniture styles—including Queen Anne (p. 78, no. 3), Chippendale (p. 78, no. 5), and Hepplewhite (p. 79, nos. 6-7).

The late 18th and early 19th centuries saw great strides in the development of the American clock industry, particularly in New England. Benjamin Willard headed the famous Massachusetts clockmaking family, with his younger brothers Simon, Ephraim, and Aaron. They produced many types— tall case (p. 79, no. 7), banjo (p. 80, no. 5), lyre, lighthouse (p. 77, no. 5), and girandole (p. 80, no. 4). Simon was the most notable because of his patented (1802) banjo clock. By inventing standardized or interchangeable wooden parts for his timepieces Eli Terry, another New Englander, became the father of the modern clock. He made possible such inexpensive clocks as the box or cottage clock (p. 77, no. 3), which by the middle of the 19th century brought the timepiece into the home of the common man.

SHELF AND MANTEL

1. French, Provincial, 18th century, lyre form. **(C)**
2. French, Louis XVI, 1774-92, gilded bronze and statuary marble. **(B)**
3. American, c. 1838, by Chauncey Jerome, ogee case. **(G)**
4. American, 1818-22, by Eli Terry, pillar-and-scroll case. **(D)**
5. American, 1820s, by Simon Willard, lighthouse type, columnar mahogany case and octagonal base. **(B)**
6. American, 1810-30, columnar case and mirror. **(F)**
7. American, 1840s, acorn mantel or shelf clock, rosewood, painted glass. **(C)**

1

2

3

4

5

6

7

TALL CASE

1. French, Louis XIV, 1643-1715, regulateur, ebonized case. **(A)**
2. American, early 1700s, by Gawen Brown, flat-top case. **(A)**
3. American, Queen Anne, 1725-50, paneled case, bonnet top with finials. **(B)**
4. American, mid-1700s, New York State, walnut case, domed top and finials. **(B)**
5. American, Chippendale, 1750-75, walnut case, pediment top. **(B)**

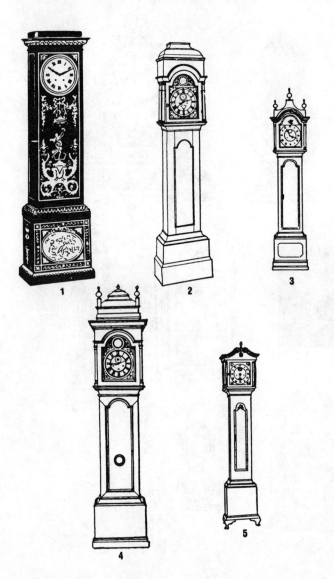

6. American, Hepplewhite, 1785-95, mahogany case, fan inlay, bonnet top. **(C)**
7. American, Hepplewhite, 1780-1800, by Simon Willard, bonnet top. **(A)**
8. American,1800-10, New England; half-high, dwarf-tall, or grandmother type; bonnet top. **(B)**
9. American, Pennsylvania-German, early 1800s, inlaid case, bonnet top. **(B)**
10. American, Shaker, early 1800s, simple paneling and molding, flat-top case. **(C)**

WALL

1. French, Louis XV, 1723-74, gilded bronze. **(A)**
2. American, 1780-90, by Simon Willard, mahogany case, exposed brass bell, finials. **(A)**
3. American, Shaker, early 1800s, walnut case, clear glass panels in door. **(C)**
4. American, 1816-32, by Lemuel Curtis, girandole type timepiece, eagle finial. **(A)**
5. American, 1830s, by Simon Willard, banjo type, stenciled case and base panel. **(A)**
6. American, 1830s, banjo type, stenciled case and base panel, eagle finial. **(B)**
7. American, 1840s, spool-turned frame, mirror-type clock, corner rosettes. **(D)**

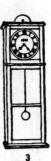

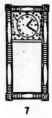

Cradles/Cribs

GENTLY moving cradles—the most primitive merely wooden boxes with attached rockers—have soothed infants since ancient times. The calming effect of a swaying cradle is of primary importance. Less critical, except perhaps to the proud parents, is the material used in such a tiny bed's construction, and the nature of its decoration. So important were such embellishments to French and English royalty that their princelings often boasted two cradles; one, encrusted with priceless jewels and gold leaf, was reserved for ceremonial appearances; the other, of much humbler design, was in everyday use in the nursery. Whatever the design or workmanship, however, most cradles were made in one of two basic ways: either suspended to swing from a supporting frame (no. 1), or attached to rockers (nos. 2 and 3). Less common was the cradle rocker pictured in no. 4, which enabled baby and mother to rock in comfort together.

Cribs with high, protective sides, such as the Victorian Cottage design in no. 5, have practically eliminated the use of cradles. Of a more practical, utilitarian nature, cribs can serve infants and toddlers alike, making the cradle, whose solace is soon outgrown, all but obsolete.

1. Cradle, Hudson Valley, 18th century, suspended on turned trestle-foot frame, painted. **(D)**
2. Cradle, 18th century, wood hoops and rails. **(D)**
3. Cradle, Pennsylvania-German, c. 1800, walnut, scalloped and pierced ends. **(E)**
4. Cradle rocker, Hitchcock style, early 1800s, arrow splats. **(F)**
5. Crib, Victorian cottage, 1850-80, spool-turned legs and spindles, vase-turned finials. **(F)**

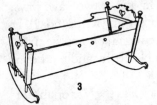

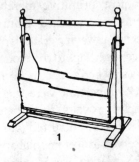

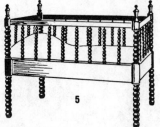

Cupboards

THE first cupboards were so named because of their structure and function: they were nothing more than open frames fitted with boards or shelves to hold cups, and were often built into a wall. As furniture craftsmen became more sophisticated, so did these simple pieces. The first corner cupboards, such as those pictured on p. 84, were usually hung from the walls; later designs were freestanding. Usually intended for use in kitchens, these pieces were fitted with doors to keep out dust and grease. Sometimes glass panels were set in so that china and glassware could be displayed to best advantage. Smaller wall cupboards, such as the American spice cupboard on p. 87 (no. 1), were designed to be hung from the kitchen walls. Freestanding pieces like the American pie safe (no. 7), were also found in the kitchen; their front panels were often made of tin to protect foods from rodents and other pests, and perforated to allow air to circulate within. Other freestanding cupboards, from the simplest Shaker design to more elaborate styles, usually incorporated both shelving and either enclosed storage or drawers, making them extremely useful pieces that could serve a variety of functions in any room in the house.

Court cupboards became popular during the 17th century. These usually consisted of elaborately carved open shelves, or a combination of shelving and enclosed storage area, such as the examples on p. 85, which could hold both utensils and bottles of wine. Press cupboards, like those illustrated on the same page, were fitted with solid doors and drawers and usually contained either shelves for linen or pegs for hanging clothes. The most massive and detailed of these pieces, beautifully carved of mahogany or oak, were found only in the wealthiest homes.

CORNER

1. French, Régence, 1715-23, paneled, decorated with brass inlay. **(C)**
2. American, Queen Anne, 1725-50, built-in, arched top. **(C)**
3. French, Louis XIV, Provincial, painted floral decoration, cabriole legs. **(D)**
4. American, Chippendale, 1750-75, broken pediment top, bracket feet. **(C)**
5. American, 1760-1800, New England, painted interior dome, arched top, flush base. **(C)**
6. French Provincial, c. 1800, two-part, glazed doors, paneled, flush base. **(D)**
7. American, Pennsylvania-German, 1790-1830, built-in, reeded, rosetted columns, flush base. **(C)**

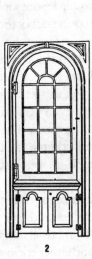

1

2

3

4

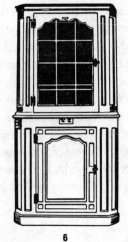

5

6

7

COURT/PRESS

1. English court cupboard, Jacobean, 1600-60, oak, melon-bulb supports. **(D)**
2. American court cupboard, 1660-80, oak split spindles, vase-turned supports, ball feet. **(B)**
3. American court cupboard, 1670-90, Virginia, white oak and yellow pine, walnut trim. **(C)**
4. American press cupboard, 1660-90, oak, two sections with lower part recessed. **(B)**
5. American press cupboard, 1660-90, oak, raised panels, sawtooth decoration, bulb-turned supports. **(B)**

1

2

3

4

5

FREESTANDING

1. American cupboard, 18th century, New England, pine, carved and paneled. **(D)**
2. American water bench, 18th-19th centuries, New England, pine. **(D)**
3. American cupboard, 1780-1850, New Jersey, pine, two sections, glass-paned upper doors. **(C)**
4. American open-face dresser, Pennsylvania-German, 1750-1840, scrolled side pieces, paneled base. **(D)**
5. American open-face dresser, 1730-1850, New England, flat overhanging cornice, butterfly hinges. **(D)**
6. American open-face dresser, 1730-1840, New England, pine, scrolled side pieces. **(E)**
7. American pie safe, Pennsylvania-German, 1780-1870, pine, perforated-tin door panels. **(E)**
8. American drug cupboard on slant-front desk, early 1800s, New England. **(D)**
9. American sill cupboard, Shaker, 1800-60, one-door cupboard set back on chest base. **(C)**

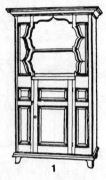

1

2

3

4

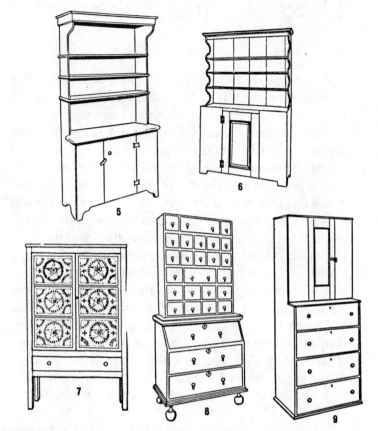

WALL

1. American spice cupboard, 1750-1800, sunken molded panel, split spindles, painted red. **(F)**
2. American cupboard, late 1700s, North Carolina, poplar, heart and tulip motifs. **(E)**
3. American cupboard, Pennsylvania-German, 1750-1820, wax inlay. **(D)**

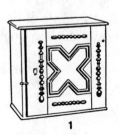

Desks/Writing Tables

Slant-topped writing boxes containing papers and other valuables were used by scribes and the educated in ancient Egypt and China; the box, portable and kept easily at hand, could be set on a table or held in the lap. Writing boxes continued to be used until the late medieval period, especially by monks. Sometime in the 12th or 13th century, the slant-topped boxes began to be mounted on three- or four-legged stands and thus became desks. As time went on the box was built on top of a chest of drawers to provide greater storage space, and the hinges were moved from the top of the slant-front to the bottom so that the desk opened outward, forming a larger writing surface. In America, the simple desk-on-chest-on-frame was common in colonial times (p. 89, no. 1). More sophisticated desks with cabriole legs, arched pigeon holes, and ornate brasses were common in America, England, and France in the 18th and early 19th centuries. During the reign of Louis XV, the fall-front desk began to become popular (p. 95, no. 10); considered a more architectural form, the fall-front remained fashionable into the late Victorian era (p. 92, no. 21).

Writing tables, sometimes called flat-top desks in English and American parlance, often have a space for the knees in the middle and drawers or cabinets to either side (p. 93, no. 1). French writing tables are often more delicate and ornate in appearance (p. 96, no. 17) than their counterparts made in other countries, though dainty writing tables with drawers in the frieze can also be seen in the American Duncan Phyfe design (p. 91, no. 13) and the English Sheraton-style lady's writing table (p. 93, no. 5).

AMERICAN

1. Desk-on-chest-on-frame, New England, early 1700s, block-and-turned legs. **(C)**
2. Desk-on-frame, William and Mary, 1690-1725, pine and maple, stretcher base, turned legs. **(D)**
3. Slant-top desk, William and Mary, 1690-1725, walnut, ball feet, teardrop drawer pulls. **(D)**
4. Desk-on-frame, Queen Anne, 1725-50, shaped skirt, cabriole legs. **(D)**
5. Desk-on-frame, Queen Anne, New England, 1725-50, shaped skirt, cabriole legs. **(C)**

6. Desk, Chippendale, New England, 1750-75, block front, butterfly brasses. **(C)**
7. Kneehole desk, Chippendale, Newport, R.I., 1750-75, by Edmund Townsend, block front with shells. **(B)**
8. Slant-top desk, Chester County, Pa., 1750-80, walnut with inlay. **(C)**
9. Slant-front desk-on-chest, New England, 1725-80, maple and walnut, arched-top pigeonholes. **(C)**
10. Tambour desk, Boston, 1780-1800, by John Seymour, satinwood. **(D)**
11. Tambour desk, Hepplewhite, 1780-1800, inlay door with tambours on each side. **(E)**

6

7

8

9

10

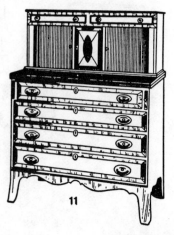

11

12. Tambour desk, Hepplewhite, 1780-1800, tambours on each side of compartment, veneer and inlay. **(E)**
13. Writing table, Duncan Phyfe, 1792-1815, hinged lid, hemispherical wells, trestle support. **(E)**
14. Desk, Sheraton, Philadelphia, 1790-1810, mahogany and satinwood. **(D)**
15. Flat-topped desk, Victorian Gothic, 1830-50, carved front panels with heraldic devices. **(F)**
16. Deaconess' desk, Shaker, early 1600s, pine writing box, curly maple tripod base. **(E)**
17. Schoolmaster's desk, New England, early 1800s, pine, slant-front desk on square frame. **(F)**
18. Davenport, Victorian Rococo, 1840-60, carved front legs. **(F)**

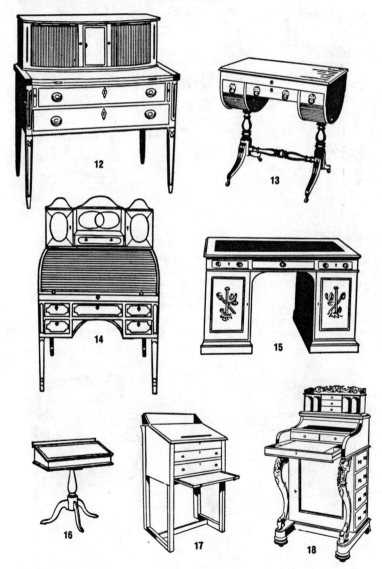

19. Drop-front desk with whatnot, Victorian Rococo, 1840-60, carved legs. **(F)**
20. Cylinder-top desk, Eastlake, 1870-1900, black walnut, incised decoration, veneer panels. **(E)**
21. Fall front desk, Victorian, 1880s, bamboo, paneled with grass matting. **(F)**

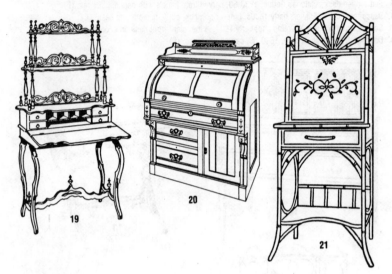

19   20   21

ENGLISH

1. Flat-topped desk, early Georgian, 1720-60, walnut with walnut veneer. **(C)**
2. Writing table, Chippendale, 1777-90, mahogany, simple inlay. **(D)**
3. Cylinder-top bureau-desk, mid-Georgian, c. 1790, inlaid satinwood. **(E)**
4. Lady's desk, Hepplewhite, 1780-1800, burl insets on cabinet panels. **(E)**
5. Lady's writing table, Sheraton, 1790-1810, rosewood, enamel plaques, brass mounts. **(E)**
6. Writing and games table, Sheraton, 1790-1810, mahogany, fluted legs, octagonal top. **(F)**
7. Pedestal desk, mid-Georgian, c. 1760-1810, in style of Thomas Shearer, mahogany, inlay, serpentine shape.
   (D)

1   2

FRENCH

1. Writing table, Louis XIV, 1643-1715, elaborate marquetry on drawer fronts and legs, cross stretchers. **(C)**

2. Writing table, Louis XIV, 1643-1715, by André Charles Boulle, inlay. **(B)**
3. Writing table, Louis XIV, 1643-1715, ebony, Boulle-type decoration, cross stretchers. **(C)**
4. Writing table, Louis XV, 1723-74, cabriole legs, shaped skirt. **(E)**
5. Slant-front desk, Louis XV, 1723-74, walnut, paneled drawers, slant front. **(D)**

6. Slant-front desk, Louis XV, 1723-74, slant front, serpentine drawer, cabriole legs. **(D)**
7. Writing table, Louis XV, 1723-74, ebony, bronze doré mounts, cabriole legs. **(E)**
8. Cylinder-top desk, Louis XV, 1723-74, geometric inlay, bronze doré handles, feet, ε d mounts. **(D)**
9. Lady's desk, Louis XV, 1723-74, drawers at back raised by a spring, cabriole legs. **(E)**
10. Fall-front desk, Louis XV, 1723-74, fall front, marquetry decoration, cabriole legs. **(D)**
11. Tambour desk, Louis XVI, 1774-92, tambour doors, tapered and fluted legs. **(E)**

12. Fall-front desk, Louis XVI, 1774-92, fall front, ceramic plaque in center. **(E)**
13. Writing table, Louis XVI, 1774-92, mahogany, inlay, bronze doré mounts, fluted and tapered legs. **(E)**
14. Writing table, Louis XVI, 1774-92, two drawers, marquetry trim. **(D)**
15. Writing table, Louis XVI, 1774-92, mahogany, gilded bronze rim, tapered legs. **(D)**
16. Cylinder-top desk, Louis XVI, 1774-92, inlay, tapered legs. **(D)**
17. Writing table, Directoire, 1795-1804, gilded copper frame color print on top. **(F)**

Highboys/Lowboys

THE highboy (called tallboy in England) developed in that country in the late 17th century as an adaptation of the chest of drawers, but never became as popular there as it did across the Atlantic, where American furniture makers quickly adopted the piece as their own. The highboy consisted of two pieces of furniture—a low stand with tall legs, generally having several drawers, which was topped by a multi-drawered chest. The most popular styles throughout the 1700s were William and Mary, Queen Anne, and especially Chippendale, with its elaborate carving, cabriole legs, and claw and ball feet. Common woods selected for the highboy were walnut and mahogany, and artisans often embellished their pieces with carved rosettes or rococo leaf ornaments. Drawer pulls were selected to harmonize with the chosen style and were often as ornate as the detailing they complemented.

The lowboy (called a dressing or side table in England) was essentially designed like the bottom portion of a highboy, and was often created to be a companion piece to it. Once again, William and Mary, Queen Anne, and Chippendale were the favored styles. The lowboy's convenient size and useful storage drawers made it popular as either a side table in the drawing room, or more often as a dressing table in the bedchamber, where it could be topped by a freestanding looking glass.

HIGHBOYS

1. American, William and Mary, 1690-1725, two-sections, burl veneer faced drawers, teardrop pulls. **(D)**
2. American, William and Mary, 1690-1725, japanned, black lacquer and gilt, trumpet-turned legs. **(C)**
3. American, Queen Anne, 1725-50, flat top, cabriole legs. **(D)**
4. American, Queen Anne, 1725-50, burl walnut, flat top, cabriole legs, cartouche-shaped mounts. **(D)**
5. American, Chippendale, 1755-80, walnut, broken-arch bonnet top, cabriole legs, shell carving. **(C)**
6. American, Chippendale, 1755-80, broken-arch bonnet top, cabriole legs, fluted corner columns. **(C)**

LOWBOYS

1. English, William and Mary, 1690-1700, trumpet legs, shaped skirt. **(D)**
2. American, William and Mary, 1690-1725, walnut, shaped skirt, acorn drops, serpentines cross stretcher. **(D)**
3. American, Queen Anne, 1725-50, shaped top, cabriole legs, slipper feet. **(D)**
4. American, Chippendale, 1755-80, elaborate carving, cabriole legs, ball and claw feet. **(C)**

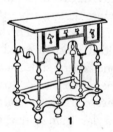

Mirrors

ACCORDING to Greek mythology, Narcissus fell in love with his reflection in a pool of water. Cleopatra, no less self-involved, probably checked her appearance in a piece of polished metal or ivory before welcoming Caesar to her chambers. Silvered glass, not unlike that used today, was introduced in Florence in the mid 1500s. The earliest mirrors—called looking glasses until the beginning of the 19th century—were quite small, as the glass was rare, available only in small pieces, and very expensive. The frames, therefore, became the embellishment. Usually of carved wood, they were gilded, or inlaid, and often decorated with fantastic rococo designs. Some, such as the Louis XV looking glass on page 104 (no. 1), incorporated colorful paintings as part of their decoration. The style of such decoration quite commonly followed popular design in furniture; thus the overwhelming popularity of Chippendale and Hepplewhite designs from the 1750s to the early 1800s was reflected in mirror treatment on both sides of the Atlantic (see pp. 101 and 103, nos. 3-7 and 7-10 respectively). In America, the patriotic Federal style usually inspired great carved eagles set atop the mirrors' crests (p. 102), while the simpler Sheraton designs were generally characterized by the use of two or more pieces of glass framed independently (p. 102, nos. 12 and 13).

AMERICAN

1. Looking glass, William and Mary, 1690-1725, veneered wood frame, pierced crest. **(F)**
2. Looking glass, William and Mary, 1690-1725, molded pine frame, fretwork crest. **(F)**
3. Mirror, Chippendale, 1755-80, mahogany frame, gilded side draperies, foliage, and bird. **(F)**
4. Dressing glass, Hepplewhite, 1780-1800, shield-shaped frame, brack feet, drawer in base. **(G)**
5. Mirror, Hepplewhite, 1780-1800, urn top, gilded metal flowers. **(F)**
6. Mirror, Hepplewhite, 1780-1800, mahogany and gilt frame, painted upper glass panel. **(G)**
7. Mirror, Hepplewhite, New England, 1780-1800, urn ornament and side leaves. **(F)**
8. Convex mirror, Federal, Duncan Phyfe, 1792-1815, gilded pine frame, spread eagle. **(E)**
9. Girandole mirror, Federal, 1785-1815, gold-leaf wood frame, eagle pediment, candleholders. **(E)**
10. Mirror, Federal, New England, c. 1800, cornice frame, painted eagle on glass panel. **(F)**
11. Mirror, Federal, New York, c. 1800, gold-leaf cornice frame, eagle pediment. **(G)**
12. Mirror, Sheraton, Massachusetts, 1790-1810, gilded cornice frame, painted upper panel. **(G)**
13. Tabernacle mirror, Sheraton, 1790-1810, flat molded cornice frame, reeded double corner columns. **(F)**
14. Courting mirror, New England, c. 1800, painted glass frame. **(F)**

1

2

3

4

5

6

7

8

ENGLISH

1. Looking glass, William and Mary, 1690-1700, inlaid frame. **(F)**
2. Looking glass, Queen Anne, 1700-20, molded frame, arched and scrolled top. **(F)**
3. Pier mirror, Queen Anne, 1700-20, gilded gesso frame, S-scrolls. **(F)**
4. Mirror, early Georgian, 1720-60, carved and gilded wood frame, broken pediment. **(E)**
5. Mirror, early Georgian, 1720-60, carved and gilded wood frame, broken pediment. **(E)**
6. Mirror, early Georgian, 1720-60, walnut frame with crest carving. **(E)**
7. Mirror, Chippendale, 1750-90, gilded gesso frame, rococo carving. **(E)**
8. Mirror, Chippendale, 1750-90, pine frame with gesso relief, gilded overall. **(E)**
9. Mirror, Chippendale, 1750-90, carved and gilded frame, phoenix crest. **(D)**
10. Mirror, Hepplewhite, 1780-1800, urn and flower motifs. **(E)**
11. Pier glass, mid-Georgian, 1760-1810, carved and gilded frame. **(F)**
12. Girandole mirror, Sheraton, 1790-1810, carved and gilded frame, eagle pediment. **(E)**
13. Mirror, Sheraton, 1790-1810, painted and gilded, cornice frame, painted upper glass panel. **(F)**
14. Convex mirror, Regency, 1795-1820, gilt frame, decorative pediment. **(F)**

FRENCH

1. Looking glass, Louis XV, Provincial, 1723-74, painting at top. **(E)**
2. Mirror, Louis XV, 1723-74, carved and gilded frame and pediment. **(F)**
3. Mirror, Louis XV, 1723-74, carved and gilded frame and pediment. **(F)**
4. Mirror, Louis XVI, 1774-92, carved and painted frame and decoration. **(F)**
5. Mirror, Directoire, 1795-1804, carved and gilded frame. **(G)**
6. Overmantel mirror, Empire, Provincial, 1804-14, cornice frame, painted upper glass panel. **(G)**
7. Cheval glass, Empire, 1804-14, ormolu mounts, candleholders. **(E)**

Secretaries

A secretary is usually a piece of furniture made in two parts, the bottom containing drawers and perhaps an open or enclosed writing area and the top comprising shelves. The earliest English or American secretary of the 17th century is a chest set on a table, such as the example (no. 1) illustrated on p. 109. This form soon evolved into the combination bureau and cabinet or bookcase, as illustrated (no. 1) on p. 106. It is this style which has persisted in popularity for the past 250 years. The most beautiful secretaries have elegant carving and make use of rare inlays. The top may feature finials and scrolled pediments. These elements are particularly noticeable in English and American Chippendale and Sheraton pieces. One of the unusual features sometimes appearing in American Federal or Sheraton secretaries is the tambour—sliding shutters which open horizontally, as in the example (no. 9) illustrated on p. 107, or roll up vertically. This same device was used in 19th-century desks (see pp. 90-91). Later secretaries are usually flat-topped rather than pedimented, but they are often no less ornamented than 18th-century pieces. Illustrated on p. 108 are two masterpieces of 19th-century design (nos. 13 and 15).

French secretaries differ greatly in design from Anglo-American examples. The typical French secretary is of one-piece with a fall front. Called either a desk or secretary, according to its size, it was sometimes copied by English cabinetmakers, as witness the Chippendale model (no. 3) shown on p. 106.

AMERICAN

1. Desk and bookcase, William and Mary, 1690-1725, walnut, arched doors, swan's neck crest. **(B)**
2. Fall-front desk on chest, William and Mary, 1690-1725, heavy top molding, teardrop handles. **(D)**
3. Small bureau desk, Chippendale, 1775-80, satinwood, inlaid. **(D)**
4. Secretary, Chippendale, New England, 1755-80, mahogany, bombé or kettle base, swan's neck crest. **(C)**
5. Block-front secretary, Chippendale, 1755-80, carved shells, vertical panels, swan's neck crest. **(D)**
6. Secretary, Hepplewhite, 1780-1800, mahogany, diamond-shaped glass cabinet panes. **(C)**

7. Secretary, Hepplewhite, 1789-1800, satinwood, cylinder front, glass panels in cupboard top. **(D)**
8. Secretary, Federal, Baltimore, 1790-1815, drapery-carved frame, pierced swan's neck crest. **(D)**
9. Tambour secretary, Federal, New England, 1780-1815, by John Seymour, Gothic-arch panels. **(C)**
10. Secretary, Sheraton, 1790-1810, mahogany, turned and reeded legs, brass finials, Gothic-arch panels. **(D)**

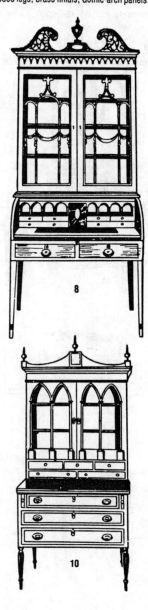

11. Lady's secretary, Sheraton, 1790-1810, fall-front desk, cupboard with Gothic-arch panels. **(D)**
12. Secretary, Federal, Salem, Mass., c. 1800, cylinder-top base, painted glass doors. **(C)**
13. Secretary, Empire, 1815-40, mahogany, brass mounts, winged-paw feet, marble corner columns. **(C)**
14. Trustee's desk, Shaker, mid-1800s, pine, twin writing surfaces, cupboards, and shelves. **(C)**
15. Secretary, Eastlake, 1870-1900, black walnut, often fitted with a roll-top rather than cupboard. **(E)**

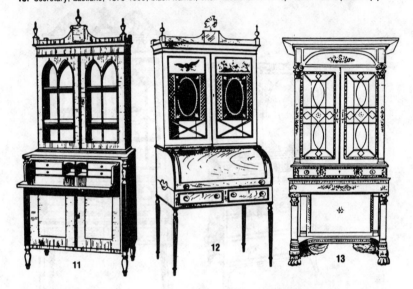

ENGLISH

1. Fall-front secretary, Restoration, 1660-90, marquetry, spiral turnings. **(B)**
2. Secretary, Queen Anne, 1700-20, simple arch paneling, swan's neck crest, slant front. **(B)**
3. Secretary, Queen Anne, 1700-20, arched panels, slant front, broken pediment top, bracket feet. **(C)**
4. Secretary, Chippendale, 1750-90, bombé or kettle base, ball and claw feet, broken pediment. **(B)**
5. Break-front secretary, Chippendale, 1750-90, mahogany, broken pediment top, flush cabinet base. **(B)**
6. Secretary-bookcase, Sheraton, 1790-1810, Gothic-arch panel doors, urn finials. **(D)**
7. Secretary-bookcase, Sheraton, 1790-1810, mahogany and satinwood, mirror door. **(D)**

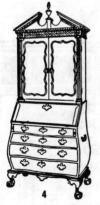

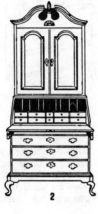

6

7

FRENCH

1. Fall front secretary, Louis XV, 1723-74, floral and geometric marquetry. **(D)**
2. Fall-front secretary, Provincial, late 1700s, fruitwood, bureau front. **(E)**
3. Fall-front secretary-bookcase, Louis XVI, 1774-92, mahogany. **(D)**
4. Fall-front secretary, Louis XVI, 1774-92, ebony and lacquer, bronze doré trim. **(D)**
5. Fall-front secretary, Empire, 1804-15, marble top, gilded bronze column mounts. **(E)**

1

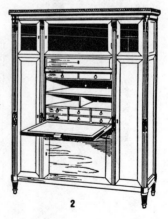

2

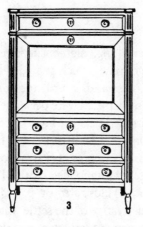

3

4

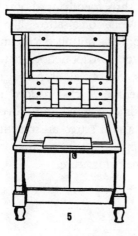

5

Settees/Settles

THE first English settles were long, high-backed, heavy wooden benches, usually made of pine, which provided little in the way of comfort, but did offer seating for three or four persons. Occasionally these massive pieces were permanently fixed; more often they were positioned near the fire in a sitting room, where their solid backs afforded some protection from cold winter drafts. Usually such pieces provide extra storage space in boxes beneath the seats, as exemplified by the 19th-century American derivative (no. 1) illustrated on p. 113.

A more popular and lasting derivative of the settle was the settee, which could usually accommodate two people in relative comfort (or sometimes, as in the case of the French petit canapés illustrated on p. 117, three friends for whom close proximity was not a problem). While some settees, like the bow-backed Windsor (no. 4) on p. 113, continued to be made entirely of wood, it became more common for upholstery to be added. Frames were beautifully carved of walnut, mahogany, or beechwood; seats (and sometimes backs) padded and covered in fine fabrics, or sometimes painted and gilded to elegant effect. While the terms "sofa" and "settee" are sometimes confused, the former generally applies to a later, larger, and more generously upholstered piece of furniture.

AMERICAN

1. Settle, early 1800s, walnut and black leather, box seat concealed chest. **(E)**

2. Settee, Hepplewhite, 1780-1800, painted decoration, square, tapering legs. **(D)**

3. Settee, Federal, 1785-1815, painted black with gilt floral motif, Gothic-arch splats, carved seat. **(D)**

4. Bow-back settee, Windsor, 1750-1815, painted, turned stretchers and legs. **(D)**

6. Settee, Windsor, Sheraton styling, 1790-1810, painted medallions; turned spindles, legs, and stretchers. **(D)**
7. Settee, Duncan Phyfe, 1792-1815; reeded mahogany frame, upholstered; outscrolled sides. **(E)**
8. Window seat, Duncan Phyfe, 1792-1815, carved rosettes, paw feet, brass casters, outscrolled sides. **(E)**
9. Settee, Victorian, 1830s-40s; mahogany frame, upholstered; scrolled back, arms, and legs. **(E)**

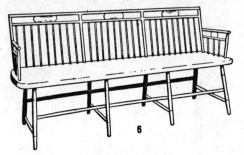

6

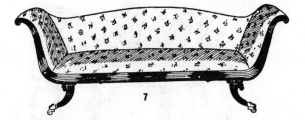

7

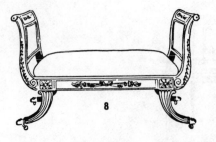

8

9

10. Settee, Victorian Renaissance, 1855-75, carved walnut frame; upholstered back, arms, and seat. **(F)**

11. Settee, Victorian, 1850s-80s, cast iron, slatted seat, back and trestle supports in fern pattern. **(F)**

12. Settee, Victorian, 1890-1910, woven wicker, upholstered seat with cushion. **(G)**

10

11

12

ENGLISH

1. Settee, Queen Anne, 1700-20, walnut frame, upholstered, cabriole legs. **(D)**
2. Settee, Queen Anne, 1700-20, two-chair-back type, walnut, scrolled arm, cabriole legs. **(D)**
3. Settee, early Georgian, 1720-60, gilded beechwood frame with shell, scroll, and acanthus leaf carving. **(D)**
4. Settee, Chippendale, 1750-90, mahogany, carved ribbon back, cabriole legs. **(D)**
5. Settee, Sheraton, 1790-1810, japanned beechwood frame, caned back and seat, polychrome decoration. **(D)**

FRENCH

1. Canapé, Régence, 1715-23, oak, caned back and seat, loose pad. **(D)**
2. Love seat, Louis XVI, 1774-92, carved and painted frame, brocade upholstery. **(E)**
3. Petit canapé, Directoire, 1795-1804, lyre back, striped upholstery. **(E)**
4. Petit canapé, Directoire, 1795-1804, mahogany, modified lyre back, loose cushion. **(E)**
5. Petit canapé, Directoire, 1795-1804, mahogany frame, upholstered, saber legs. **(E)**

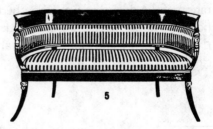

Sideboards

THE sideboard evolved, as its name implies, because of the need for additional serving space near the dining table. At first a simple side table affording no storage space, it sometimes came to have a shallow central drawer for storing linens and silver. It was generally flanked by twin pedestals for storing and cooling wine, which were topped by urns holding knives. The English designer Thomas Shearer is most often credited with having blended these elements into a single unit in the latter part of the 18th century; the wine coolers were incorporated on each side of the piece, which retained its central drawer. Additional storage, as in the Hepplewhite designs on p. 119, was sometimes recessed beneath the drawer. Later adaptations, such as the elaborate Eastlake design on p. 122 (no. 16), sometimes incorporated additional open shelving or cupboards as a type of superstructure. English and French designs, and more rarely American ones, were sometimes topped with marble, which was thought to be impervious to spills. Rich woods like mahogany and satinwood were used; elaborate inlay work and carving embellished the fronts. As sideboards became more popular and homes larger, the pieces were sometimes recessed into special dining wall niches to conserve valuable floor space in the room. A uniquely-American adaptation of the sideboard was a Southern innovation: the hunt board or hunter's table was a tall sideboard designed so that the huntsmen could stand comfortably at it in their riding clothes to take refreshment.

AMERICAN

1. Serpentine-front sideboard, Hepplewhite, 1780-1800, crotch veneer, string inlay, inset panels. **(D)**
2. Serpentine-front sideboard, Hepplewhite, 1780-1800, inlay, inset panels. **(D)**
3. Serpentine-front sideboard, Hepplewhite, 1780-1800, oval and circular banding, inset panels. **(D)**

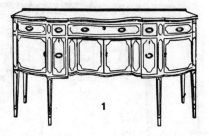

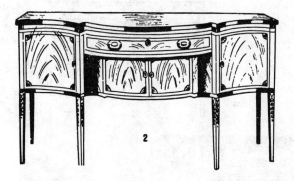

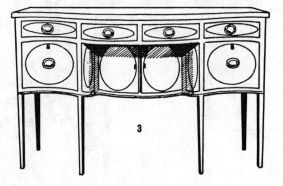

4. Serpentine-front sideboard, Hepplewhite, 1780-1815, by Mills and Deming, string inlay. **(C)**
5. Server with tambour cupboard, Hepplewhite, 1780-1800, by John Seymour, mahogany. **(C)**
6. Serpentine-front sideboard, Hepplewhite, New England, c. 1780, mahogany, inlaid, tapering legs. **(D)**
7. Serpentine-front sideboard, Hepplewhite, 1780-1800, mahogany, vase and grape inlay. **(D)**

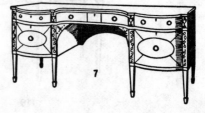

8. D-shaped sideboard with tambour cupboard, Hepplewhite, c. 1780, square tapered legs. **(D)**
9. Serpentine-front sideboard, Federal, Maryland, 1790-1815, bellflower inlay. **(D)**
10. Serpentine-front sideboard, Federal, Maryland, 1790-1815, bellflower and eagle inlays. **(D)**
11. Straight-front sideboard, Sheraton, 1790-1810, mahogany, carved, fluted, and paneled. **(D)**

12. Server, Sheraton, 1790-1810, center cupboards, side drawers. **(E)**

13. Sideboard, Empire, 1815-40, crotch veneer, drawer overhangs cabinet; carved finials, legs, feet. **(E)**

14. Sideboard, Shaker, early 1800s, walnut top, birch frame, pine doors, painted. **(C)**

15. Sideboard, Victorian Renaissance, 1855-75, marble top, paneled cupboard, back with pediment and shelf. **(E)**

16. Sideboard, Eastlake, 1870-1900; paneled cupboards, shelves, and tableware cupboard. **(E)**

12

13

14

15

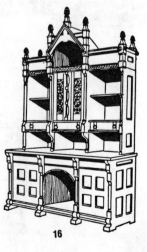

16

ENGLISH AND FRENCH

1. Sideboard, Chippendale, 1770s-90s, satinwood, inlay of grapes on frieze. **(D)**
2. Sideboard with undershelf, Louis XVI, 1774-92, marble top, bowed front. **(E)**
3. Shaped-front sideboard, Hepplewhite, 1780-1800, mahogany, string inlay, tapered legs. **(D)**
4. Semicircular sideboard, Sheraton, 1790-1810, mahogany, light-colored inlay, cellerette drawers. **(E)**
5. Sideboard, Sheraton, 1790-1810, outcurved corners, reeded posts, turned and reeded legs. **(E)**
6. Serving table, Sheraton, 1790-1810, mahogany and satinwood, reeded legs. **(E)**

Sofas

THE words "sofa" and "couch" are now used interchangeably to define a generously-proportioned, upholstered seating unit for two or more persons. A couch, however, was originally a long, half-backed lounge with a head rest, meant for solitary reclining, which is now more commonly referred to as a day bed or chaise longue. The word "sofa" comes from the Turkish word for a pile of carpets used for reclining in comfort. The term was not in general use in England before the 18th century; early sofas are sometimes hard to differentiate from settees, but usually they are larger, more generously upholstered, and less formal pieces. During the early 1800s, sofas became increasingly fashionable, and it was *de rigueur* to have at least one (or preferably two) large ones in the drawing room to facilitate conversation or aid relaxation, as they were frequently used for lounging. The tête-à-tête style, illustrated on p. 127 (no. 13), became the rage at mid-century: a rather twisted love seat, it was basically two chairs facing in opposite directions whose joined backs formed an "S" curve. Often framed in lustrous mahogany or rosewood, sofas in simple, sophisticated styles like the Sheraton pieces on pp. 125 and 126, or with lavish carved accents, such as the mermaid leg supports featured in the mid-Georgian sofa on p. 128 (no. 2). Most 18th- and 19th-century styles, however, had in common their wedding of beautiful woods to fine upholstery: the frame and supports were as important as the stuffing. Modern imitators too often hide inferior legs and framing beneath billows of fabric.

AMERICAN

1. Hepplewhite, 1780-1800, camel back, serpentine back, roll-over arms, tapered legs. **(C)**
2. Federal, Baltimore, 1790-1815, concave back, bellflower carvings on tapered legs. **(D)**
3. Sheraton, 1790-1810, concave back, reeded arms and legs. **(E)**
4. Sheraton, 1790-1810, straight back, mahogany frame, cornucopia and wheatsheaf carvings, reeded front legs. **(D)**

5. Sheraton, 1790-1810, curved back rail, maple frame, vase-shaped front legs and arm supports. **(E)**

6. Sheraton, 1780-1815, by Samuel McIntire, carved back panel, vase-shaped front legs and arm supports. **(D)**

7. Sheraton, Maryland, 1790-1810, raised and curved back rail, vase-shaped arm supports, tapered legs. **(D)**

8. Duncan Phyfe, 1792-1815, Récamier style, carved frame, outscrolled high end, scrolled lower end. **(E)**

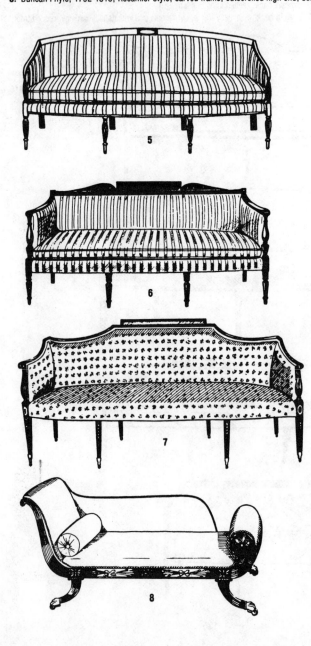

9. Duncan Phyfe, 1792-1815, double-lyre style, outscrolled arms, plain crest rail, ornamental legs. **(D)**

10. Victorian Rococo, 1840s-60s, medallion-back, carved serpentine back frame, cabriole legs. **(F)**

11. Victorian Rococo, 1840s-60s, medallion-back; finger-molded, lightly-carved, continuous frame. **(F)**

12. Victorian Rococo, 1840s-60s, rosewood frame, scroll and foliage carving. **(E)**

13. Victorian Rococo, 1840s-60s, tête-à-tête form, laminated rosewood frame, cabriole legs. **(E)**

14. Victorian Rococo, 1840s-60s, méridienne, carved mahogany frame. **(F)**

15. Victorian Renaissance, 1855-75, in the style of Louis XVI, needlework upholstery. **(E)**

16. Victorian, 1880-1900, circular form, ottoman or ''sociable,'' flat center pedestal for a plant. **(F)**

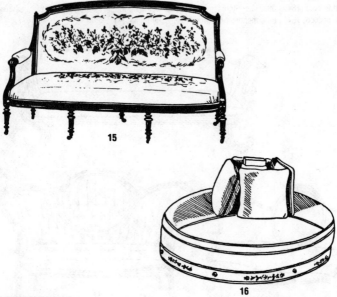

15

16

ENGLISH

1. Mid-Georgian, 1760-1810, carved and gilded frame, upholstered seat and back, outscrolled arms. **(D)**

2. Mid-Georgian, 1770-90, by John Linnell, mermaid figure leg supports, outscrolled arms. **(B)**

3. Hepplewhite, 1780-1800, continuous-bow back and arms, tapered front legs, fluted arm supports. **(E)**

4. Hepplewhite, 1780-1800, straight back, painted frame with bellflowers.. **(D)**

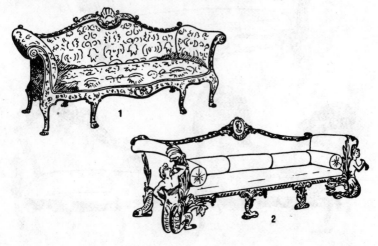

1

2

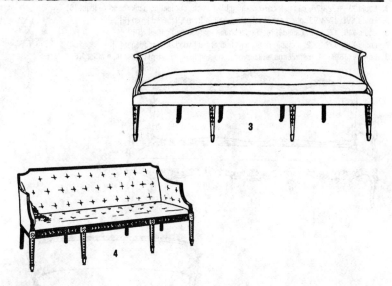

FRENCH

1. Louis XV, 1723-74, marquise (small sofa), continuous-bow back and arms, cabriole legs. **(D)**
2. Louis XV, 1723-74, canapé, carved and gilded frame, serpentine back and arms, cabriole legs. **(D)**
3. Louis XV, 1723-74, ottomane, oval form, gilded wood, incurved arms, cabriole legs. **(D)**

4. Louis XV, 1723-74, canapé, carved and gilded wood, serpentine back, cabriole legs. **(D)**
5. Louis XVI, 1774-92, ottomane, oval form, walnut frame, tapered legs. **(E)**
6. Louis XVI, 1774-92, canapé, rectilinear frame, carved and gilded. **(D)**
7. Louis XVI, 1774, 92, canapé, rectilinear frame, fruitwood, tapered legs. **(E)**
8. Empire, 1804-14, méridienne, outcurved arms and legs, one arm higher than other. **(E)**

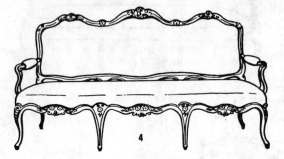

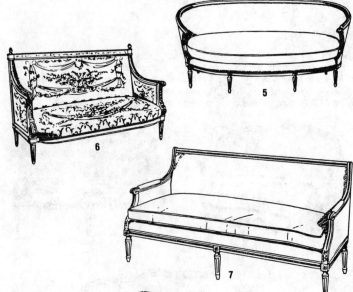

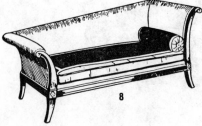

Stands

ORNAMENTAL stands for clothing, hats, umbrellas, plants, vases, and washing accessories became very popular in the 19th century. While some of the most elaborate pieces are now very expensive, the typical small antique stand is reasonably priced today. It is also one of the most utilitarian of period furnishings. Washstands are often used now as night or dressing tables; marble-topped stands that once held Victorian knick-knacks (p. 133, no. 4) make convenient lamp tables. Hall and dressing stands continue to be used as intended and are wonderfully-worked creations. Some include a place for shoes, clothing, hats, and umbrellas; others are more specialized in function. Almost all have at least several arms and incorporate a small oval mirror and a tray where personal items may be placed. Cast iron was often used for the hall stand which stood in the front hallway near the main entrance. It may be as conveniently used today in the bedroom as a dressing stand.

The only type of stand which is not included in the following pages is the candlestand. This was the most common type of stand used in the early American home, and a separate section, pp. 31-32, is devoted to its varied forms.

DRESSING AND HALL STANDS

1. Hall stand, American, Victorian Gothic, 1830s-50s, carved wood, pegs, small mirror, umbrella racks. **(E)**
2. Hall stand, American, Victorian Gothic, 1830s-50s, quatrefoil and crocket carving, marble shelf. **(E)**
3. Dressing stand, Austrian, mid-1800s, by Thonet, bentwood frame and support for mirror, bentwood table. **(F)**
4. Hall stand, American, Victorian Rococo, 1840s-60s, cast iron, umbrella drip pan, small mirror. **(F)**

WASHSTANDS

1. American, Hepplewhite, 1780-1800, corner form, storage shelf, drawer, shaped back and skirt. **(F)**
2. American, Sheraton, 1790-1810, corner form, storage shelf, drawer, shaped back and skirt. **(F)**
3. American, Shaker, early to mid-1800s, pine, galley on one side and back, three drawers and cupboard. **(E)**
4. American, Victorian Cottage, 1850s-80s, spool-turned legs and towel bars, one drawer, gallery. **(G)**

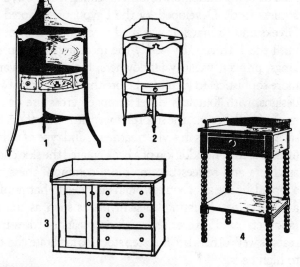

OTHER FORMS

1. Urn stand, English, Hepplewhite, 1780-1800, mahogany, fluted legs, scalloped top. **(F)**
2. Stand for plant or lamp, American, Victorian, mid-late 1800s, Mother-of-pearl inlaid and gilded. **(F)**
3. Stand for vase or lamp, Victorian Renaissance, 1855-75, painted removable top. **(G)**
4. Stand for plant or vase, Victorian Renaissance, 1855-75, marble top and shelves, lower glass shelf. **(G)**

Stools

The oldest and simplest form of seating is the low, backless, armless stool. Developed by the Egyptians, adapted by the Greeks and Romans, it was used throughout Europe as well until the 17th century. Only the most important persons— kings, princes, wealthy landowners, high clergy—warranted more sophisticated furniture before the 1600s. In its two basic designs, with four legs either arranged crosswise or at right angles from the seat, the stool changed little over the centuries, save for differences in style, treatment, and type of upholstery (if any) used. The addition of a back created the side chair, and as chairs and settees became more common, the stool was adapted for use as a footrest, often designed to harmonize with a larger type of seating. Elegant pieces such as the French tabourets (p. 135) were used as window seats and dressing-table seats as well; others became step stools to facilitate climbing into high beds.

Often designed in conjunction with other pieces of furniture, and upholstered to match armchairs or side chairs, the handsome cabriole-legged Queen Anne style, one of the most popular (no. 4), was usually intended as a footrest. Joint stools (nos. 1-3) were first common during the Jacobean era, and are usually characterized by their turned legs (and, originally, by their mortise and tenon joints).

AMERICAN AND ENGLISH

1. Joint stool, American, Pilgrim Century, c. 1650, turned legs and feet. **(E)**
2. Joint stool, American, Pilgrim Century, late 1600s, turned legs and feet. **(E)**
3. Joint stool, American, New York City, early 1700s, white oak, carved rails and stretchers. **(E)**
4. Stool, English, Queen Anne, 1700-20, upholstered top, cabriole legs. **(E)**
5. Stool, English, early Georgian, 1720-60, mahogany, fabric top, scrolled sides, cabriole legs. **(D)**
6. Rectangular stool, English, Sheraton, 1790-1810, mahogany, turned legs and stretchers, fabric top. **(F)**
7. Tabouret, American, Victorian, late 1800s, hexagonal top and sides, wood inlay, Moorish arches. **(G)**

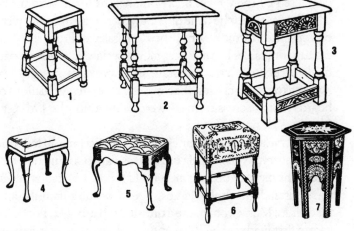

FRENCH

1. Tabouret, Louis XIV, 1643-1715, serpentine cross stretcher, petit point top. **(E)**
2. Tabouret, Louis XV, 1723-74, carved and gilded, cabriole legs, upholstered top. **(F)**
3. Tabouret, Louis XVI, 1774-92, bowed front, fluted banding, tapered legs. **(F)**
4. Tabouret, Louis XVI, 1774-92, painted and gilded, tapered legs. **(F)**

TABLES

Small four-legged tables were common among the inventive people of ancient Egypt. Though tables of various sorts were used by the Greeks and Romans, the form faded in the Middle Ages, and the table did not return as an ordinary piece of household furniture until the Renaissance. From the 15th century on, tables became ever more specialized and were particularly popular and elaborate in upper-class households. Among the lower classes, the simplest tables—constructions of boards placed across trestles—were in use until the 19th century (p. 153, nos. 1-8).

Over the last three centuries tables have become an intrinsic part of everyday life. Their uses are as varied as function dictates. The night or bedside table (p. 137, nos. 1-5) stands beside the bedstead and holds lamps, books, writing utensils, and medicines. Many women use a dressing table (p. 142, nos. 1, 2), a form first made in the 18th century, as a place to keep jewelry and cosmetics and to apply make-up. Tables for dining vary greatly in form. Among the most common types are the butterfly and gate-leg (pp. 137-38, nos. 1-4); center, a popular Victorian form (pp. 138-39, 1-12); hutch or chair (p. 142, nos. 1, 2); tavern/stretcher, a popular 18th-century form (p. 151, nos. 1-6); trestle, with a plank top (p. 153 nos. 1-8); and various plain dining tables, some with extensions (pp. 140-41, nos. 1-8). Occasional tables (pp. 143-44, nos. 1-12), and side, sofa, library, pier, and console tables (pp. 147-50, nos. 1-28) are spread throughout the house and serve as catchalls for one's belongings. Tea tables (p. 152, nos. 1-9) provide a special place to hold tea sets used in formal afternoon teas.

The only other common form of table—the card table—is treated separately (pp. 33-37). In both form and use it differs from those illustrated here.

BEDSIDE/NIGHT TABLES

1. French, Louis XVI, 1774-92, open shelf, cabriole legs. **(F)**
2. English, Sheraton, 1790-1810, satinwood, pierced tray top, paneling, inlay stringing. **(E)**
3. American, Federal, 1785-1815, by John Seymour, two drawers, columnar fluted legs. **(E)**
4. American, Sheraton, 1790-1810, mahogany and satinwood, scalloped shelf, two drawers. **(F)**
5. American, Victorian Cottage, 1850s-80s, maple, spool-turned legs, one drawer. **(G)**

BUTTERFLY/GATE-LEG TABLES

1. Gate-leg table, American, William and Mary, 1690-1725, with drawer, eight legs, four gates. **(C)**
2. Gate-leg table, American, William and Mary, 1690-1725, walnut, eight legs, two gates. **(D)**
3. Butterfly drop-leaf table, American, William and Mary, 1690-1725, maple, canted legs. **(D)**
4. Butterfly drop-leaf table, American, William and Mary, 1690-1725, canted legs. **(D)**

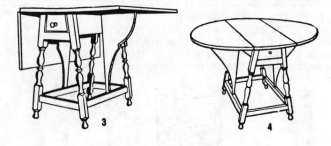

CENTER TABLES

1. French, Louis XIV, 1643-1715, carved and gilded, legs in form of fantastic animals. **(B)**
2. French, Directoire, 1795-1804, walnut, partly painted, tripod base. **(E)**
3. English, Regency, 1795-1820, drum form, tripod base, hexagonal pillar, paw feet. **(E)**
4. French, Empire, 1804-14, mahogany, ebony and boxwood inlay, lion-paw feet. **(E)**
5. American, Empire, 1815-40, pedestal base, marble top, brass paw feet. **(E)**

6. American, Victorian, 1830s-40s, scrolled pedestal, serpentine marble top. **(F)**
7. American, Victorian Rococo, 1840s-60s, by François Seignouret, rosewood, leaf-carved legs, hoof feet. **(E)**
8. American, Victorian Rococo, 1840s-60s, by John Belter, laminated rosewood, detailed carving. **(C)**
9. American, Victorian Rococo, 1840s-60s, Belter type, black walnut, marble top, scrolled and carved. **(E)**
10. American, Victorian Cottage, 1850s-80s, black walnut pedestal, white marble top. **(F)**
11. Austrian, Victorian, mid-1800s, Thonet, bentwood pedestal, solid oval top. **(F)**
12. American, Eastlake, 1870-1900, oak, pillar support, extension leaves. **(F)**

CORNER TABLES

1. American, William and Mary, 1690-1725, Virginia, three legs, one gate. **(E)**
2. English, Queen Anne, 1700-20, one drop leaf, cabriole legs. **(F)**

DINING TABLES

1. English, Queen Anne, 1700-20, walnut, drop leaf, straight legs, pad feet. **(D)**
2. English, early Georgian, 1720-60, mahogany, drop leaf, cabriole legs. **(D)**
3. English, Chippendale, 1750-90, drop leaf, two swing legs, carved cabriole legs with claw-and-ball feet. **(E)**
4. American, Hepplewhite, 1780-1800, Maryland, two drop-leaf banquet tables, swing legs. **(C)**
5. American, Hepplewhite, 1780-1800, one of two banquet tables, eagle and bellflower inlay. **(C)**
6. American, Duncan Phyfe, 1792-1815, breakfast table, drop leaf, cluster column support. **(E)**
7. American, Duncan Phyfe, 1792-1815, extension table, two curved four-leg supports. **(D)**
8. American, Empire, 1815-40, extension table, three pedestals, spiral-reeded shafts. **(D)**

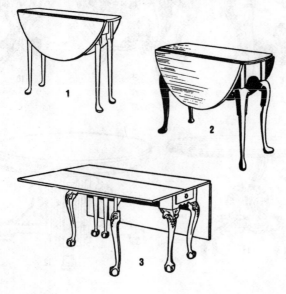

DRESSING TABLES

1. English, Hepplewhite, 1780-1800, form known as Beau Brummel, fitted interior, lid top. **(E)**
2. American, Victorian Rococo, 1840s-60s, by Prudent Mallard, marble top, X-stretcher. **(D)**

HUTCH TABLES

1. American, William and Mary, 1690-1725, hinged circular top, drawer in seat, turned legs. **(D)**
2. American Queen Anne, 1725-50, chestnut, box seat; turned arms, legs, and stretchers. **(E)**

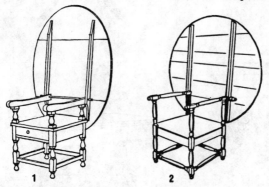

OCCASIONAL TABLES

1. English, Queen Anne, 1700-20, walnut and mahogany, low molding dish top. **(E)**
2. French, Louis XV, 1723-74, chiffonier, two drawers. **(F)**
3. French, Louis XV, 1723-74, table en haricot (kidney-shaped table), cabriole legs. **(E)**

4. English, Chippendale, 1750-90, for displaying china, mahogany, marble top, claw-and-ball feet. **(E)**
5. American, Country, New England, 1750-1840, pine, half-round, square legs. **(G)**
6. English, Sheraton, 1790-1810, rosewood, drum top, tripod base. **(E)**
7. English, Sheraton, 1790-1810, mahogany, kidney-shaped, square, tapering legs. **(F)**
8. American, Shaker, mid-1800s, oval pine top and base, birch turned legs. **(F)**
9. American, Victorian Cottage, 1850s-80s, trestle-type, spool-turned uprights, scrolled feet. **(G)**
10. American, Victorian Renaissance, 1855-75, pillar-and-cross base, inlaid top, angular braces. **(F)**
11. American, Eastlake, 1870-1900, pink and chocolate marble top, black walnut base with incising. **(G)**
12. American, Eastlake, 1870-1900, walnut, gingerbread apron, beveled edges. **(G)**

PEMBROKE TABLES

1. American, Chippendale, 1750-90, narrow drop leaves, drawer, fluted legs. **(E)**
2. American, Hepplewhite, 1780-1800, narrow drop leaves, drawer, inlay. **(F)**
3. American, Hepplewhite, 1780-1800, narrow drop leaves, drawer, bellflower inlay, brass ankle bands. **(E)**
4. American, Hepplewhite, 1780-1800, narrow drop leaves, drawer, inlay stringing. **(F)**
5. American, Federal, 1790-1815, Maryland, narrow drop leaves, drawer, inlay stringing. **(E)**
6. American, Duncan Phyfe, 1792-1815, serpentine drop leaves, drawer, reeded legs. **(F)**
7. English, Sheraton, 1790-1810, satinwood, narrow drop leaves, shaped top, drawer. **(F)**

SEWING/WORK TABLES

1. Worktable, French, Louis XVI, 1774-92, drawer and two shelves, turned supports. **(E)**
2. Architect's table, French, Louis XVI, 1774-92, mahogany, leather top, brass trim. **(E)**
3. Sewing table, English, Hepplewhite, 1775-1800, splayed legs, two drawers, fabric bag. **(F)**
4. Sewing table, American, Sheraton, 1790-1810, raised top, one drawer, fluted legs. **(F)**
5. Sewing table, American, Sheraton, 1790-1810, New York City, octagonal, carved pedestal. **(F)**
6. Worktable, American, Duncan Phyfe, 1792-1815, tripod base, acorn drops, three drawers. **(E)**
7. Worktable, American, Duncan Phyfe, 1792-1815, tambour front, hinged top, writing board. **(E)**
8. Sewing table, American, Duncan Phyfe, 1792-1815, octagonal, tambour front, pedestal base. **(E)**

9. Sewing table, American, Federal, c. 1800, Salem, Mass., octagonal, fabric bag. **(E)**
10. Sewing table, American, Federal, 1800-10, New York City, hinged top, end compartments. **(F)**
11. Worktable, American, Empire, 1815-40, by Charles-Honoré Lannuier, hinged top, writing board. **(D)**
12. Sewing stand, American, Shaker, early 1800s, pine, painted, cutting board. **(D)**
13. Worktable, American, Shaker, early 1800s, birch, two drawers, tripod base. **(D)**
14. Bake-room table, American, Shaker, c. 1840, pine, painted, high counter, drawers, and shelf. **(D)**
15. Sewing table, American, Shaker, mid-1800s, mixed woods, drop leaf at back, overlapping top. **(D)**

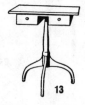

SIDE, SOFA, LIBRARY, PIER, AND CONSOLE TABLES

1. Side table, English, Restoration, 1660-90, marquetry trim, spiral-turned legs, curved X-stretcher. **(D)**

2. Console, French, Louis XIV, 1643-1715, carved and gilded wood, marble top. **(D)**

3. Side table, English, Queen Anne, walnut base, marble top, cabriole legs. **(E)**

4. Library table, English, early Georgian, 1720-60, by William Kent, lion-head terminals and shells. **(B)**

5. Side table, English, early Georgian, 1720-60, carved and gilded pine, cabriole legs. **(D)**

6. Side table, English, early Georgian, c. 1730, mahogany, marble top, carved cabriole legs. **(D)**

7. Console, English, early Georgian, 1720-60, gilded support, marble top. **(C)**
8. Side table, English, early Georgian, 1720-60, by William Kent, gilded pine base, marble top. **(C)**
9. Console, French, Louis XV, 1723-74, shell carving, cabriole legs. **(D)**
10. Console, French, Louis XV, 1723-74, carved and gilded. **(C)**
11. Side table, English, Chippendale, 1750-90, inlaid satinwood top, carved and gilded base. **(E)**
12. Side table, English, Chippendale, 1750-90, carved and gilded pine. **(E)**
13. Console, English, Robert Adam, 1765-95, demilune shape, painted and inlaid. **(D)**
14. Pier table, English, mid-Georgian, 1760-1810, carved and gilded, inlaid marble top. **(D)**
15. Side table, English, Robert Adam, 1765-95, carved and gilded, marble top. **(E)**

16. Sofa table, English, Sheraton, 1790-1810, satinwood, spiral-reeded legs and stretcher. **(E)**

17. Pier table, American, Duncan Phyfe, 1792-1815, gilt mounts; turned, tapered, and reeded legs. **(E)**

18. Library table, American, Duncan Phyfe, 1792-1815, drop leaf, carved urn pedestal. **(E)**

19. Sofa table, American, Duncan Phyfe, 1792-1815, urn-shaped supports, acanthus carving. **(D)**

20. Sofa table, American, Empire, early 1800s, by Charles-Honoré Lannuier, mahogany, eagle decoration. **(C)**

21. Console, American, Empire, early 1800s, by Charles-Honoré Lannuier, caryatid supports. **(C)**

22. Console, French, Directoire, 1795-1804, painted and gilded, marble top. **(E)**

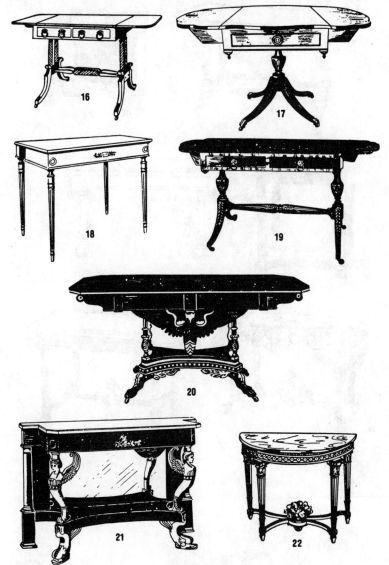

23. Sofa table, American, Empire, early 1800s, drop leaf, curved bracket supports, caryatid supports. **(D)**
24. Console, American, Empire, 1815-40, mahogany, marble top and columns, back mirror panel. **(E)**
25. Console, French, Provincial, Empire, 1804-14, brass mounts, marble top. **(E)**
26. Sofa table, American, Victorian Gothic, 1830s-50s, walnut, drop leaves, bracket feet, column supports. **(E)**
27. Console, American, Victorian Rococo, 1840s-60s, marble top, cabriole legs, shell-carved knees. **(E)**
28. Side table, American, Victorian Renaissance, 1855-75, marquetry wood top, carved column legs. **(F)**

23

24

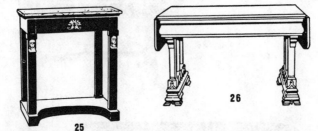

25

26

27

28

TAVERN/STRETCHER TABLES

1. American, 18th century, pine, stretcher base, turned legs and feet. **(E)**
2. American, New England, 18th century, oak and pine, oval top, canted legs, box stretcher. **(E)**
3. American, New England, early 1700s-1820, pine, octagonal top, stretcher base. **(E)**
4. American, Southern, early 1700s, yellow pine top, cypress legs and H-stretcher. **(E)**
5. American, New England, 18th century, heart-and-scroll carved skirt, turned legs, two drawers. **(E)**
6. American, Southern, 18th century, cherry, stretcher base with knob turnings. **(E)**

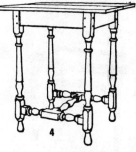

TEA TABLES

1. American, William and Mary, 1690-1725, arched scalloped skirt, stretcher base. **(E)**
2. American, Queen Anne, 1725-50, tray top, cabriole legs. **(E)**
3. American, Chippendale, 1750-75, tray top, gadrooned skirt, cabriole legs, claw-and-ball feet. **(E)**
4. English, Chippendale, 1750-90, gallery top, used for display of silver. **(E)**
5. English, Chippendale, 1750-90, octagonal top with gallery, tripod base. **(E)**
6. American, Chippendale, 1750-75, tip-and-turn table, piecrust edge, tripod base. **(E)**
7. French, Directoire, 1795-1804, mahogany tilt top, gilded-bronze gallery. **(E)**
8. French, Directoire, 1795-1804, serving table, inlay design, gilded-bronze gallery. **(E)**
9. American, Victorian, late 1800s, tilt top, papier-mâché design with gilt and mother-of-pearl inlay. **(F)**

TRESTLE AND SAWBUCK TABLES

1. Sawbuck table, American, New England, 17th-19th centuries, maple trestle and X-shaped supports, pine top. **(E)**
2. Trestle table, American, New England, c. 1680, two-board top, turned stretcher and uprights. **(D)**
3. Sawbuck table, American, Pennsylvania, early 18th-19th centuries, oak and walnut, drawer. **(E)**
4. Trestle table, American, Pennsylvania, early 18th-19th centuries, cut-out supports with wedges. **(E)**
5. Trestle table, American, Country, late 18th-mid-19th centuries, oak frame, maple top. **(F)**
6. Trestle table, American, Shaker, 19th century, pine top, birch trestles. **(D)**
7. Trestle table, American, Shaker, 19th century, pine top on hardwood, X-trestles, for ironing. **(D)**
8. Trestle table, American, Shaker, 19th century, pine top, birch trestles, for communal dining. **(C)**

Wardrobes/Armoires

IT is thought that the wardrobe or armoire was first produced in the Middle Ages in response to the need for a place to store arms and armor. In the 16th and 17th centuries, the armoire was modified to hold clothes, and, as a piece of household furniture, it began to be produced in more and more elaborate and heavily embellished versions. By the 19th century, when wardrobes were used by almost everyone, many had drawers in the bottom and mirrors attached to the doors.

In the 17th century, French armoires began to be intricately carved and inlaid, since they were used as the clothes chests of the upper classes (pp. 155-56, nos. 1,4,5,6). American wardrobes did not reach the same level of sophistication until the early 19th century (p. 157, no. 10). Instead, earlier wardrobes often reflect the origins of the settlers in the areas in which they were built. The kas (p. 155, nos. 2,3) was made in New York City and the Hudson Valley area by colonists of Dutch descent. It is lower and more simply made than its French counterpart; but its handsome splayed cornice, carved or painted doors, and ball feet make it a prized piece today. The schrank, the type of wardrobe built by the Pennsylvania Germans, is taller and narrower than the kas, but is often carved or decorated in much the same manner (p. 156, nos. 7,8). As the closet did not come into widespread use in America until the late 19th century and is still not ubiquitous in Europe, the armoire remains an important and decorative piece of furniture, especially appropriate for those occupying older houses.

1. Armoire, French, Louis XIV, 1643-1715, ebony, Boulle style inlay decoration. **(C)**

2. Wardrobe, American, Hudson Valley, early 1700s, oak and gumwood, elaborate paneling. **(C)**

3. Wardrobe, American, New York City, early 1700s, painted, deep cornice, ball feet. **(C)**

4. Armoire, French, Régence, 1715-23, paneled, carved and inlaid, bronze doré trim. **(D)**

1

2

3

4

5. Armoire, French, Louis XV, 1723-74, oak, rococo carving. **(E)**

6. Armoire, French, Louis XV, 1723-74, two parts, paneled doors, flat top. **(E)**

7. Wardrobe, American, Pennsylvania-German, late 1700s, walnut, paneled, painted heart motif. **(C)**

8. Wardrobe, American, Pennsylvania-German, late 1700s, walnut, inlay trim. **(C)**

9. Wardrobe, American, Empire, 1815-40, carved and gilded rosewood, paneled doors. **(D)**

10. Wardrobe, American, Empire, 1815-40, carved and gilded rosewood, paneled doors. **(D)**

5

6

7

8

9   10

Whatnots/Étagères/Vitrines

In the 19th century, when the collecting of china, rocks, fossils, and all manner of curios, bibelots, souvenirs, and geegaws was a popular pastime among the leisured classes, whatnots, vitrines, and étagères became immensely popular pieces of furniture as they provided places to exhibit these prizes. Eighteenth-century examples of vitrines, whatnots, and étagères can be found, though they are much rarer than later pieces. Whatnots and étagères usually consist of a series of three or four shelves supported by three or four columns often intricately carved. Such fine woods as walnut and rosewood were sometimes employed in the construction. With the advent of the jigsaw in the mid-1800s, the scrollwork became even more elaborate than it had been earlier in the century. Vitrines, on the other hand, are much simpler pieces. Rather than being open like whatnots and étagères, vitrines are enclosed cases with shelves inside and glass panels on the front, sides, and top. Cases of this type are generally used in museums or to house collections in the home that must be kept dust free. Today books and records and even hats and gloves are stored in pieces of furniture of these three types. Often designed to be placed in a corner, they do not take up useful space and cannot be easily upset.

1. Vitrine, French, Directoire, 1795-1804, adjustable glass shelves, pediment top. **(E)**
2. Whatnot, American, Sheraton, New York City, c. 1810, two display shelves, Canterbury section. **(F)**
3. Whatnot, American, Victorian Gothic, 1830s-50s, Gothic tracery shelves, Gothic-paneled base. **(F)**
4. Étagère, American, Victorian Rococo, 1840s-60s, mirror in rosewood frame, graduated shelves, marble base. **(F)**
5. Whatnot, American, Victorian Cottage, 1850s-80s, black walnut, spool-turned uprights. **(H)**
6. Whatnot, American, Victorian Cottage, 1850s-80s, black walnut, carved crest, turned uprights. **(H)**

NOTES

NOTES

NOTES

NOTES